A Years Bird Extremadura – what to see and when to see it.

By Ian Parsons

Introduction

Extremadura in central western Spain is rightly known as one of *the* birding destinations in Europe. With a very low human population and vast tracts of countryside, the bird species found here are found in numbers that other places in Europe can only dream of: Almost 50% of the European population of the European Black Vulture and 12% of the entire global population of Great Bustard are found in Extremadura.

The region is also a stronghold for two Iberian endemics, namely the Iberian Azure-winged Magpie and the Spanish Imperial Eagle. Both of these iconic species of Europe's avifauna can be found with ease in this birding paradise.

With a list of bird species that will make any birder drool, plus the abundance of cheap flights to Spain, it is no wonder that many, many European bird watchers head to the region every year. Extremadura is big though, with many different habitats and, of course, many of the desired bird species are migratory and not present all year round. Winter species like Common Crane arrive in late October and are going again at the beginning of March. Some spring and summer migrants can start to arrive by the end of January whilst others don't arrive until May. The timing of your visit is just as important as where you visit.

This book is written to help you get the most out of your visit, whatever time of year you make it. If you are visiting in April or November, the first part of the book will tell you what species are present, what species will be arriving and what species will be departing. It also highlights which of the many habitats can be the most rewarding during the month, enabling you to plan ahead as to where you will go. Excerpts from my diaries for each month also give you a flavour of what can be seen.

The second part of the book looks at the main habitats associated with the region, the birds and other wildlife associated with them and where the best examples of the habitat can be found. It also details key birding areas and the habitats that can be found there, as well as providing a list of target species to look for whilst exploring them. A small sample of Extremadura's star birds are covered in more detail, each one referring back to the key birding areas where you can find them. Finally there is a section on the people and culture of Extremadura and on driving in the region, all important information for the visitor to know. Throughout the second part of the book you will find helpful birding tips, written from direct experience, which should ensure that you get the most from your time in Extremadura.

Every birder has to visit Extremadura; quite simply it is a brilliant place. Enjoy!

Part 1

-Month by month guide to the species of Extremadura

Resident Birds

Extremadura has over 100 resident species of bird. Some are ubiquitous and found throughout the region, others are more specific in their habitat. The Alpine Accentor can only be found at the highest altitudes whilst the Purple Swamphen can only be found at a handful of lowland wetland sites.

Extremadura, particularly Cáceres province, has a diverse wealth of habitats and it is easily possible to drive for a couple of hours and pass through habitat that will hold many of the residents species listed below.

Note: Some of these species were formerly considered migratory but, in recent years, they are increasingly found all year round. A good example is the Little Bittern, which although much more common in the spring and summer, is now over wintering in increasing numbers each year.

1	Gadwall
2	Mallard
3	Red-legged Partridge
4	Little Grebe
5	Great Crested Grebe
6	Great Cormorant
7	Little Bittern
8	Night Heron
9	Cattle Egret
10	Little Egret
11	Great Egret
12	Grey Heron
13	White Stork
14	Black-winged Kite
15	Red Kite
16	Griffon Vulture

17	Black Vulture
18	Marsh Harrier
19	Goshawk
20	Sparrowhawk
21	Common Buzzard
22	Spanish Imperial Eagle
23	Golden Eagle
24	Bonelli's Eagle
25	Common Kestrel
26	Peregrine Falcon
27	Water Rail
28	Moorhen
29	Purple Swamphen
30	Common Coot
31	Little Bustard
32	Great Bustard
33	Black-winged Stilt
34	Stone Curlew
35	Little Ringed Plover
36	Black-bellied Sandgrouse
37	Pin-tailed Sandgrouse
38	Rock Dove/Feral Pigeon
39	Woodpigeon
40	Collared Dove
41	Barn Owl
42	Eagle Owl
43	Little Owl
44	Tawny Owl
45	Long-eared Owl
46	Kingfisher
47	Hoopoe
48	Iberian (Green) Woodpecker
49	Great Spotted Woodpecker
50	Lesser Spotted Woodpecker
51	Calandra Lark
52	Crested Lark

53	Thekla Lark
54	Woodlark
55	Crag Martin
56	Grey Wagtail
57	White Wagtail
58	Dipper
59	Wren
60	Dunnock
61	Alpine Accentor
62	Robin
63	Black Redstart
64	Stonechat
65	Black Wheatear
66	Blue Rock Thrush
67	Blackbird
68	Mistle Thrush
69	Cetti's Warbler
70	Zitting Cisticola
71	Blackcap
72	Dartford Warbler
73	Sardinian Warbler
74	Long-tailed Tit
75	Crested Tit
76	Coal Tit
77	Blue Tit
78	Great Tit
79	Nuthatch
80	Short-toed Treecreeper
81	Penduline Tit
82	Iberian Grey Shrike
83	Jay
84	Azure-winged Magpie
85	Magpie
86	Red-billed Chough
87	Jackdaw
88	Carrion Crow

89	Raven
90	Spotless Starling
91	House Sparrow
92	Spanish Sparrow
93	Tree Sparrow
94	Rock Sparrow
95	Red Avadavat
96	Common Waxbill
97	Chaffinch
98	Serin
99	Greenfinch
100	Goldfinch
101	Linnet
102	Hawfinch
103	Cirl Bunting
104	Rock Bunting
105	Corn Bunting

Whilst some of the residents can be scarce and have very local distributions (Carrion Crow being one of them) others are abundant. The following species are the ten most common birds found in the region:

House Sparrow
Spotless Starling
Crested Lark
Barn Swallow
Corn Bunting
Goldfinch
Blue Tit
Azure-winged Magpie
Spanish Sparrow
Chaffinch

Although sometimes a controversial topic – taxonomists seldom agree with one another! – the following is a list of Iberian endemic and 'near endemic' resident species and subspecies that can be found in Extremadura.

Red-legged Partridge	*Alectoris rufa hispanica*
Spanish Imperial Eagle	*Aquila adalberti*
Pin-tailed Sandgrouse	*Pterocles alchata alchata*
Eurasian Eagle Owl	*Bubo bubo hispanus*
Iberian Green Woodpecker	*Picus sharpie*
Crested Lark	*Galerida cristata pallid*
Thekla Lark	*Galerida theklae theklae*
Bluethroat	*Luscinia svecica azuricollis*
Black Redstart	*Phoenicurus ochruros aterrimus*
Black Wheatear	*Oenanthe leucura leucura*
Pied Flycatcher	*Ficedula hypoleuca iberiae*
Long-tailed Tit	*Aegithalos caudatus irbii*
Coal Tit	*Periparus ater vierae*
Blue Tit	*Cyanistes caeruleus ogliastrae*
Great Tit	*Parus major corsus*
Eurasian Nuthatch	*Sitta europaea hispaniensis*
Iberian Grey Shrike	*Lanius meridionalis meridionalis*
Eurasian Jay	*Garrulus glandarius fasciatus*
Azure-winged Magpie	*Cyanopica cooki*
Eurasian Magpie	*Pica pica melanotos*

Along with the residents, the region also boasts large numbers of migratory birds, be they wintering like the Common Crane or breeding like the Roller. Others use the region as a prolonged stopover on their journey, such as the Pied Flycatcher, which seems to be everywhere during September and October. The month by month guide lists all these migrants, showing when they arrive, when they are present and when they depart. Birds that have an extended passage period, meaning that they are present for more than a week or two, are recorded as migrants arriving, with their departure shown in the month when the passage period ends. Those passage migrants that pass through quickly are listed as on passage. A good example of this is the Pied Flycatcher, pre-breeding passage is in April and lasts about a week, so for the month of April the bird is listed as on passage. The Pied's post breeding passage however, is a much more extended affair starting in August and lasting right through until November. Therefore in August the bird is listed under Migrants Arriving, for September and October it is listed under Migrants Present and in November it is listed under Migrants Departing.

For each month a 'Small bird to see' is also suggested; it is easy to be drawn by the larger birds on show, but it is important not to miss out on the smaller species. The species suggested are easy to see, but generally unobtrusive and can be missed or, in the case of the Thekla Lark, mistaken for something else.

Every month also has a Potential Mega; the very nature of a Mega means, of course, that you are unlikely to see the species in question, but all of the species listed have turned up in Extremadura in their month so you never know...

A brief description is given on what the weather for the month generally is, followed by a summary of the migrant movement. Various habitats that are good to visit in the month are suggested as well as a brief summary of what some of the species found in them are doing.

The diary excerpts for each month are taken from my diary covering the years 2012 and 2013.

January

Migrants Present

Greylag Goose; Wigeon; Teal; Pintail; Shoveler; Pochard; Tufted Duck; Black-necked Grebe; Hen Harrier; Merlin; Common Crane; Golden Plover; Lapwing; Dunlin; Snipe; Curlew; Greenshank; Green Sandpiper; Stock Dove; Skylark; Meadow Pipit; Water Pipit; Bluethroat; Fieldfare; Song Thrush; Redwing; Chiffchaff; Goldcrest; Firecrest; Common Starling; Brambling; Siskin; Bullfinch; Reed Bunting. (34)

Migrants Arriving

Common Sandpiper (1)

Migrants Departing

None

On Passage

None

Total Potential Species Including Residents: 140

January can be a cold month, but on clear days the strength of the sun can be felt as it shines down. There is virtually no migration during this first month of the year other than the arrival of Common Sandpipers who grace the numerous water bodies with their bobbing tails as they feed.

This is a good month to head for the rice fields of Extremadura where you can be greeted by the birding spectacle of thousands of Common Crane as they feed around you and fill the sky over your head; their trumpeting calls echoing across the open landscape. Joining them in this watery world are thousands of Greylag Geese and Lapwings, as well as many waders and ducks. Red Avadavats and Common Waxbills are present in large groups and these, coupled with large noisy flocks of Spanish Sparrow, attract the attention of the wintering Merlins. Look out for the blur as these small falcons dash low over the rice in pursuit of their quarry.

Both Golden and Spanish Imperial Eagles can be found displaying this month, with plummeting dives from both birds being one of the birding highlights of the whole year. The Spanish Imperial Eagle is very vocal at this time of year, announcing it's presence with short, sharp barks; definitely a sound to listen out for, especially in the bird's dehesa strongholds.

Griffon Vultures start to nest this month and their nesting colonies can become very noisy as they squabble over their real estate and try and 'borrow' bits of nest material from one another. If you are lucky you may witness one of these large vultures snapping dead branches out of trees and scrub to use in the nest; they fly in towards the dead branch, grip it with their feet and rely on their momentum and weight to snap the branch off. It might not be the most elegant of procedures but it is very effective!

Out on the plains large groups of Golden Plover, Lapwing and Spotless Starlings abound. Scanning the Starlings should reveal some of their spotted cousins, the Common Starling, in amongst them. There will also be large groups of Calandra Lark, as well as their wintering cousins the Skylark. Little Bustards form large flocks at this time of year, often numbering well in to triple figures, and can put on quite a show, especially if something spooks them and they all take to the air as one, flashing their bright white wing patterns as they do so.

Small bird to see: In the winter months the Water Pipits descend from their lofty mountain retreats (many breed in the neighbouring Sierra de Gredos to the north) and can be found throughout the region, but are easily overlooked. Check the edges of the many small reservoirs that can be found on the outskirts of towns and villages for this sometimes shy Pipit. You are only likely to confuse it with the abundant Meadow Pipits at this time of year, but a good view of its less streaky paler back, striking head pattern and long bill will leave you in no doubt.

Potential Mega: The Red Knobbed Coot is a real European rarity that is only just hanging on as breeding species in a handful of sites in southern Spain. In the winter though, there is some movement of birds, with individuals occasionally turning up in Extremadura with three scattered across the region in January 2015.

January Diary Excerpts:

...we just stopped and watched in amazement as two Black Vultures flew slowly past us giving terrific close views...

...dozens and dozens of Black-headed Gulls, two Spoonbills, one of which was bathing itself vigorously. Lots of White Stork and Lapwing around the edges whilst on the water there were at least 50 Tufted Duck, 6 Shoveler, 2 Pochard and lots of Mallard...

...whilst watching this, the female Spanish Imperial Eagle appeared once more and again put on a fantastic show...

...six Griffon Vultures flew low overhead and several Azure-winged Magpies were feeding noisily in the dehesa...

...Corn Buntings sat on fence posts singing loudly and lots of Stonechats, in breeding pairs, being very territorial. A Dartford Warbler was calling and in the distance I could hear Cranes trumpeting...

...a beautiful and big Golden Eagle sat just a few metres from us. It sat staring at us for a couple of seconds before jumping up, spreading its wings and flying off...

...a group of 50 – 60 Little Bustard suddenly took flight as a Red Kite drifted past. Found 18 Black-bellied Sandgrouse flying in great light...

February

Migrants Present

Greylag Goose; Wigeon; Teal; Pintail; Shoveler; Pochard; Tufted Duck; Black-necked Grebe; Hen Harrier; Merlin; Common Crane; Golden Plover; Lapwing; Dunlin; Snipe; Curlew; Greenshank; Green Sandpiper; Common Sandpiper; Stock Dove; Skylark; Meadow Pipit; Water Pipit; Bluethroat; Song Thrush; Chiffchaff; Siskin; Bullfinch; Reed Bunting. (29)

Migrants Arriving

Black Stork; Spoonbill; Egyptian Vulture; Lesser Kestrel; Spotted Redshank; Great Spotted Cuckoo; Sand Martin; Barn Swallow; Red-rumped Swallow; House Martin. (10)

Migrants Departing

Fieldfare; Redwing; Goldcrest; Firecrest; Common Starling; Brambling (6)

On Passage

None

Total Potential Species Including Residents: 150

February can be very spring like with temperatures regularly up in the high teens. Spring migrants start to arrive whilst some of the winterers begin the journey back to their breeding grounds elsewhere.

This is a good month to visit the dehesa woodlands so abundant in the region. It is probably the best time to get good close views of Common Crane as they feed up on the acorns underneath the Evergreen Oaks. Normally they are fairly wary but, with their long migration looming, they lose some of this nervousness as they concentrate on building up their fat stores. Roving bands of Azure-winged Magpies can be seen feeding in the canopies and on the ground below, their beautiful colours flashing in the sunlight as they move from tree to tree. Hoopoe can show really well as they sit in the top of the Oaks singing their fantastic song, stating their territorial ownership to all.

This month it is also worth going to church; these huge old buildings dominate the centres of towns and villages throughout the region. They provide excellent nest sites for many species of birds including the returning Lesser Kestrels and great views can be had of this small falcon towards the end of the month as they sit up and pose above their nest entrances. The churches (and many other old buildings) are also home to White Storks; their pair bonding bill clacking display is particularly prevalent this month and well worth seeing and hearing.

White Storks at their nest

The slightly smaller Black Stork also returns to its breeding sites this month, so check out steep sided rocky river valleys as these are favourite haunts. In the sun, these river valleys also produce good conditions for soaring raptors and other large birds, providing lots of air flow and lift. Black, Griffon and the returning Egyptian Vultures can get very close to you as they all exploit this.

The heavily grazed fields on the edges of villages and towns are worth a walk around in the morning this month, there will be numerous tracks leading to them from the village or town and they are there to be used, so do so. The fields will have large numbers of Meadow Pipits feeding in them and these, in turn, attract Hen Harriers which can be seen frequently quartering the fields this month. The fences and gates of these fields play host to singing Corn Buntings that provide a jangling, pleasant soundtrack as you walk along.

Small bird to see: Black Redstarts can be found in all sorts of habitat, from urban buildings through to river valleys. This month they are particularly vocal and the male's song with its peculiar middle part is definitely something to be listening out for. Although quite a showy bird to look at, their small size and unassuming habits can mean they are sometimes overlooked especially if other, bigger, birds are around.

Potential Mega: Although the Pallid Harrier is an eastern European breeder it has been expanding its breeding range westwards in recent years and this has led to an increase in sightings of this raptor during the winter months in Spain. Extremadura is no exception and there have been a number of records in recent winters. It is still though an extremely scarce bird with only one or two individuals turning up. A real mega and one worth bearing in mind when watching the much more common Hen Harriers.

February Diary Excerpts:

…calling Sardinian and Dartford Warbler throughout, a few flocks of Linnet and absolutely loads of Serin…

…the harsh 'drrit' of House Martins, now abundant in number and the song of Barn Swallow accompanying us…

…had a Cetti's Warbler singing as well as briefly showing itself, over towards the hill a Little Owl called and a Hoopoe flew past, a group of at least 40 Azure-winged Magpie were moving…

…sat in the sun I saw an Otter swimming quite casually across the river. We had great views as it swam away from us, occasionally diving down below the surface…

…there were at least 6 Black Vultures around it and a few more Griffons, with the sky above filling up with more…

…whilst listening to the Black Redstart singing we had a couple of Hoopoe fly by and a nice group of Calandra Lark noisily flying from…

…watch the several dozen Griffon Vultures in the air as well as a pair of Black Stork, several Cormorant and my first Egyptian Vulture of the year…

…could hear lots of Cranes calling and eventually 60 of them came into view. We hadn't been there very long *when a familiar raptor shape appeared — an Imperial, it was a male and it gave fine views as it flew around stooping and 'bark' calling...*

March

Migrants Present

Teal; Pintail; Shoveler; Pochard; Black-necked Grebe; Black Stork; Spoonbill; Egyptian Vulture; Lesser Kestrel; Dunlin; Snipe; Curlew; Spotted Redshank; Greenshank; Green Sandpiper; Common Sandpiper; Great Spotted Cuckoo; Sand Martin; Barn Swallow; Red-rumped Swallow; House Martin; Meadow Pipit; Water Pipit; Chiffchaff. (24)

Migrants Arriving

Garganey; Common Quail; Purple Heron; Black Kite; Short-toed Eagle; Montagu's Harrier; Booted Eagle; Ringed Plover; Little Stint; Redshank; Wood Sandpiper; Common Cuckoo; Scops Owl; Alpine Swift; Common Swift; Pallid Swift; Short-toed Lark; Tawny Pipit; Tree Pipit; Yellow Wagtail; Northern Wheatear; Black-eared Wheatear; Savi's Warbler; Sedge Warbler; Reed Warbler; Subalpine Warbler; Willow Warbler; Woodchat Shrike. (28)

Migrants Departing

Greylag Goose; Wigeon; Tufted Duck; Hen Harrier; Merlin; Common Crane; Golden Plover; Lapwing; Stock Dove; Skylark; Bluethroat; Song Thrush; Siskin; Bullfinch; Reed Bunting. (15)

On Passage

None

Total Potential Species Including Residents: 172

March can be a month of contrasts with days of rain followed by days of sunshine. This is a month of colour with many of the regions wild flowers at their best. More migrants are arriving throughout the month, but many of the iconic wintering ones are departing.

This is a good month to visit areas of countryside interrupted by rocky ridges and interspersed with olive groves, dehesa and pasture. The swifts return this month, with Pallids arriving before Common, but it is the larger Alpine Swift that can make a visit to this habitat rewarding as they hunt above the ridge tops. Woodchat Shrikes arrive in large numbers and can be seen with ease as they establish themselves for the spring and summer. The resident Iberian Grey Shrikes have already started to breed and the males can often be found sat up surveying their territory. The characteristic call of the Common Cuckoo can be heard ringing out, whilst the harsh cackling call of the Great Spotted Cuckoo is also a frequent sound. Now is probably the best time to see the Great Spotted Cuckoo and it can often be found perched out in the open, but, as the spring rolls on, it soon becomes much harder to see well. The newly returned Booted Eagle can be seen patrolling these areas, often causing panic amongst the small birds as it does so.

Broken rocky country is also good this month, with birds like the Northern Wheatear using it as a prolonged stopping off point as they feed up for a few weeks before moving north again in April. The Black-eared Wheatear also arrives this month, but, unlike its cousin, it stays to breed; the smart males often showing really well. This is good habitat for snakes and Short-toed Eagles are often found hunting over it, using their long wings to hang in the air as they scan below.

On the plains there is a changing of the guard with the Harriers, with the Hen leaving and the Montagu's arriving. If you are lucky you can get to see both species quartering the same field at the same time. Elsewhere on the plains, the male Great Bustards, now in full breeding plumage, can be seen strutting around in preparation for the forthcoming lek.

Small bird to see: The resident Black Wheatear is not as easily found as it once was; many pairs have disappeared from what were regular sites. Steep rocky ground, typical of many of the river valleys in the region, is the best place to find them, listen out for their quiet thrush like song that can be heard this month.

Potential Mega: Little Crakes, as they move back towards their eastern European breeding grounds, occasionally get blown off course and reach Spain. Extremadura has a handful of records with the most recent being for March 2014. Wetland sites are the place to look for this diminutive rail.

March Diary Excerpts:

...Chaffinch, Serin and Cetti's Warbler singing away. I then heard a loud almost cackle like call and a few seconds later a Great Spotted Cuckoo appeared...

...there were a group of eight Lesser Kestrels hovering together over a field dominated by Lavender...

...in the distance several Griffon Vultures were circling away. We were about to move on when a beautiful male Hen Harrier appeared from nowhere and flew right across the front of us...

...a lovely view of a big 'V' of Cranes flying from the dehesa back towards their roost – about 80 of them...

...had the first Black Kite of the year followed a minute or two later by the first Short-toed Eagle of the year...

...the first Booted Eagle of the year, a pale phase bird, drifted over, as well as several Griffon Vulture, Black Kite and one Black Vulture, as well as lots of White Storks...

...One of the Black-winged Kites was sat in the top of last years nest tree, whilst its mate was perched on the pylon wire above it. Further off a Short-toed Eagle was hanging in the air hunting for snakes, nearer to me a Zitting Cisticola was performing its display flight...

Male Lesser Kestrel hovering.

April

Migrants Present

Common Quail; Purple Heron; Black Stork; Spoonbill; Black Kite; Egyptian Vulture; Short-toed Eagle; Montagu's Harrier; Booted Eagle; Lesser Kestrel; Ringed Plover; Common Sandpiper; Great Spotted Cuckoo; Common Cuckoo; Scops Owl; Alpine Swift; Common Swift; Pallid Swift; Short-toed Lark; Sand Martin; Barn Swallow; Red-rumped Swallow; House Martin; Tawny Pipit; Tree Pipit; Yellow Wagtail; Northern Wheatear; Black-eared Wheatear; Savi's Warbler; Sedge Warbler; Reed Warbler; Subalpine Warbler; Woodchat Shrike. (34)

Migrants Arriving

Honey Buzzard; Hobby; Collared Pratincole; Curlew Sandpiper; Gull-billed Tern; Turtle Dove; Bee-eater; Roller; Nightingale; Redstart; Rock Thrush; Great Reed Warbler; Melodious Warbler; Garden Warbler; Western Orphean Warbler; Whitethroat; Spectacled Warbler; Bonelli's Warbler; Spotted Flycatcher; Golden Oriole; Ortolan Bunting.(21)

Migrants Departing

Teal; Pintail; Garganey; Shoveler; Pochard; Black-necked Grebe; Little Stint; Dunlin; Snipe; Curlew; Spotted Redshank; Greenshank; Green Sandpiper; Wood Sandpiper; Meadow Pipit; Water Pipit; Chiffchaff; Willow Warbler. (18)

On Passage

Osprey; Whinchat; Pied Flycatcher. (3)

Total Potential Species Including Residents: 181

April is the month where the weather starts to stabilise into the dry sunny climate associated with this part of Spain. More migrants arrive throughout the month, including the ultimate songster, the Nightingale, whose fluid notes can be heard from seemingly every bit of scrub.

This is a good month to visit the plains, these wide open spaces provide excellent birding all year round, but this month, two of its stars are really shining. Both Great Bustard and Little Bustard lek during April; the Great Bustard males turn themselves almost inside out transforming into white foaming masses, while the Little Bustards plump up their striking black neck feathers and call from a raised piece of ground or low rock. Their call sounds just like blowing a raspberry and is incredibly far carrying despite its low pitch, it will sound a lot closer than it is so careful scanning is likely to be required to find the male. In the middle of the month the Rollers arrive and these like nothing better than sitting on the telegraph wires that often run along the roads that cross the plains.

The reed beds of Extremadura may be few and far between, but this month they are well worth visiting. The resident birds, like the fantastic Purple Swamphen and predatory Marsh Harrier, are joined by Purple Heron and the noisy Great Reed Warbler. Egrets abound and are joined by Spoonbill and in some years, Glossy Ibis.

Towards the end of the month Bee-eaters and Golden Orioles arrive bringing their vibrant colours with them. Bee-eaters can be found everywhere but Golden Orioles can be a bit more elusive and are best looked for in shallow valleys with plenty of tall trees, particularly Poplars and Planes. Another colourful bird, the resident Blue Rock Thrush can be found in valleys and rocky places, the resplendent males often singing away from an elevated sunny spot.

Golden Eagle, Spanish Imperial Eagle and Bonelli's Eagle will all have young in their nests meaning that the adults will have to be out hunting more often, giving you more chance of views of these impressive raptors.

Small bird to see: Whilst many Tawny Pipits that can be found in open habitats during the month are on extended passage a few stay to breed. These sandy coloured pipits blend in well with the tracks but they are quite confiding and can give good views.

Potential Mega: The Red-footed Falcon is a bird that normally breeds in eastern Europe but, during April, as it returns there from its wintering grounds, it is possible for a bird to get lost and turn up in Extremadura. There are only a handful of records of this small falcon but they are increasing in frequency.

April Diary Excerpts:

...several Griffon Vultures and Black Kite high up, as well as a Black Stork drifting through. A Viperine Snake was basking by the river whilst on a wire a Black-eared Wheatear was singing away...

...Birdsong was everywhere, there were several Nightingales singing away, as well as a Cetti's Warbler. In the air there were several Bee-eaters hawking...

...Gull-billed Terns calling away as they flew overhead, as well as Bee-eaters and a couple of Purple Herons. Further up, the sky was full of Griffon Vultures, Black Kites and the odd Black Vulture...

...good views of Blue Rock Thrush sunning itself, whilst Pallid and Common Swifts, as well as Red-rumped Swallows and House Martins fed in the air around it. A lovely male Black Wheatear popped up on a wall...

...had a Rock Bunting that showed really well for a couple of minutes and then a Hawfinch flew in and sat on a branch in front of us. A Hoopoe was calling constantly...

...a male Montagu's Harrier put on a real show for us for at least three minutes. I found a Great Bustard showing well and as I looked around I spotted a male Little Bustard with its neck feathers inflated...

...several very good and prolonged views of Purple Swamphens, both on the water and clambering over the reeds. A male Little Bittern took off and flew right in front of us...

Little Bittern hiding in the reeds

May

Migrants Present

Common Quail; Purple Heron; Black Stork; Spoonbill; Honey Buzzard; Black Kite; Egyptian Vulture; Short-toed Eagle; Montagu's Harrier; Booted Eagle; Lesser Kestrel; Hobby; Collared Pratincole; Gull-billed Tern; Turtle Dove; Great Spotted Cuckoo; Common Cuckoo; Scops Owl; Alpine Swift; Common Swift; Pallid Swift; Bee-eater; Roller; Short-toed Lark; Sand Martin; Barn Swallow; Red-rumped Swallow; House Martin; Nightingale; Redstart; Black-eared Wheatear; Rock Thrush; Savi's Warbler; Reed Warbler; Great Reed Warbler; Melodious Warbler; Western Orphean Warbler; Whitethroat; Spectacled Warbler; Subalpine Warbler; Bonelli's Warbler; Spotted Flycatcher; Golden Oriole; Woodchat Shrike; Ortolan Bunting. (45)

Migrants Arriving

Little Tern; Common Nightjar; Red-necked Nightjar; White-rumped Swift; Rufous Bush Robin; Red-backed Shrike. (6)

Migrants Departing

Ringed Plover; Curlew Sandpiper; Common Sandpiper; Tawny Pipit; Tree Pipit; Yellow Wagtail; Northern Wheatear; Sedge Warbler; Garden Warbler; (9)

On Passage

None

Total Potential Species Including Residents: 165

May is a month of good sunny weather with the heat gradually building as it heads towards June. The last of the spring migrants arrive this month including the rare, but increasing, White-rumped Swift.

This is a good month to head out at night to see Owls and the newly arrived Red-necked Nightjar. Many of the towns and villages will have Scop's Owls breeding in them, the small owl favours pollarded trees with holes in and many of these can be found in parks, alongside roads and around many of the churches and older buildings. Whilst looking for these you should also see Barn Owls, they are very much urban birds in Extremadura, feeding on the roosting Sparrows and Spotless Starlings. They often breed in the large old buildings so typical of the larger villages and towns. For the Nightjars, head out of town and chose a site that has a lot of low horizons to help you pick the birds up in flight. They tend to breed in scattered pine and eucalyptus clumps and these can often be found around the reservoirs on the edges of towns and villages. Listen out for their strange repeated 'ka-tok, ka-tok' song.

This is a good month to visit Monfragüe National Park (see Birding Area 4, page 111), stopping at Peňa Falcon will reward you with breathtaking views of Griffon Vultures as they circle around you. Scanning the cliff opposite the viewing areas you will see their young, now almost fully grown, sat hunched trying to keep out of the sun. There are several pairs of Black Stork breeding on this cliff, as well as on the large rocks that rise up out of the river. These beautiful birds will have young in the nest and will be making frequent visits to feed them allowing you great views of this normally hard to see species. Listen out for the distinctive alarm call of Peregrines as they too breed here, they can be hard to pick up in flight as they are dwarfed by the many huge Griffon Vultures that are constantly in the air, but careful watching should find them.

Out on the plains, the Great Bustard males will still be in their finery and it is possible to find post lek groups of males, sometimes of up to twenty birds. The areas that have been heavily grazed are now drying out rapidly; the bare patches on them are worth scanning for both Sandgrouse species who will glean tiny seeds from the dusty surface. Make sure you are out before the heat of the day otherwise the heat haze will hinder your search.

Small bird to see: The Rock Bunting is a small, unassuming bird that is easily missed but, with its beautiful head pattern, this is a bird that is well worth seeing. They can be found in many areas, but one of the best places to see them is below the viewpoints already mentioned above, in Monfragüe. The birds here are particularly confiding, so make sure you tear yourself away from the large birds all around and look down at the rocks and vegetation below you.

Rock Bunting in Monfragüe

Potential Mega: Immature Lanner Falcons have been recorded and photographed during this month in various places in Extremadura, but with records totalling less than ten for this smart falcon, this is a real mega for the region.

May Diary Excerpts:

...nice views of a Sardinian Warbler, several Spanish Sparrows and Spotless Starling in the dehesa, a few Azure-winged Magpies were moving around and another couple of Hoopoe. Watched a Woodchat Shrike chase a Crested Lark that had a beak full of caterpillars...

...at least a dozen Black-winged Stilts who were either nesting, feeding or making lots of noise! Several Bee-eaters were about as well as a very showy pair of Red-rumped Swallows...

...lots of Alpine Swift, sometimes ridiculously close, Griffon Vultures, Crested Lark and Goldfinches. We could hear Nightingale, Cetti's Warbler and Golden Oriole...

..perfect views of an Egyptian Mongoose on the way. Out on the plain the first birds were two very confiding Short-toed Larks. Corn Bunting everywhere, good close views of both Calandra Lark and Tawny Pipit as well as a couple of Montagu's Harrier...

...the Spanish Imperial Eagle barked a few times and then appeared. It came around the rock this time and flew right across the front of us, all of its markings showing brilliantly in the light...

...the Rollers were numerous and we had great views of several birds – at least 17 individuals as well as Common Kestrel, Spotless Starling, Hoopoe and a Little Owl...

...got great views of a Savi's Warbler that sat up in the reeds and 'reeled' away. A Great Reed Warbler also showed well singing right in front of us, while further off a Marsh Harrier...

Great Reed Warbler

June

Migrants Present

Common Quail; Purple Heron; Black Stork; Spoonbill; Honey Buzzard; Black Kite; Egyptian Vulture; Short-toed Eagle; Montagu's Harrier; Booted Eagle; Lesser Kestrel; Hobby; Collared Pratincole; Gull-billed Tern; Little Tern; Turtle Dove; Great Spotted Cuckoo; Common Cuckoo; Scops Owl; Common Nightjar; Red-necked Nightjar; Alpine Swift; Common Swift; Pallid Swift; White-rumped Swift; Bee-eater; Roller; Short-toed Lark; Sand Martin; Barn Swallow; Red-rumped Swallow; House Martin; Rufous Bush Robin; Nightingale; Redstart; Black-eared Wheatear; Rock Thrush; Savi's Warbler; Reed Warbler; Great Reed Warbler; Melodious Warbler; Western Orphean Warbler; Whitethroat; Spectacled Warbler; Subalpine Warbler; Bonelli's Warbler; Spotted Flycatcher; Golden Oriole; Red-backed Shrike; Woodchat Shrike; Ortolan Bunting. (51)

Migrants Arriving

None

Migrants Departing

None

On Passage

None

Total Potential Species Including Residents: 156

June is the month when the heat really starts to go up. It is a stable month bird wise, with no migrants or passage birds on the move. It can be a good month to turn up juvenile Great

Spotted Cuckoo as they leave their Common Magpie surrogates to prepare for their migration.

This is a good month to get out on the plains, but make sure you take a hat and plenty of water! The plains are dry and almost Serengeti like in appearance. Larks abound. Flocks of Calandra Lark will be in amongst the grassy vegetation and sitting up on the fence posts. Crested Larks and Short-toed Larks can be found on the tracks. Adding to the mix will be flocks of Corn Bunting and all of these small birds attract the graceful Montagu's Harrier. Every year there are a few melanistic examples of this raptor on the plains of Caceres. Aggregations of White Storks can occur; taking advantage of large numbers of large grasshoppers as they wade through the grass, bills snapping. Black Vultures can often be found loafing, sat out on the plain looking absolutely huge. In the evening stake out one of the large stock watering holes and wait to see if a Stone Curlew or one of the Sandgrouse come in for a much needed drink.

White Storks and Black Kites on the Plains

The cooler scrubby areas, often found below dams, are good places to visit if you want to see the *Sylvia* warblers and to hear and see the Nightingale. Golden Orioles can turn up in this habitat too and there should be a ready supply of Azure-winged

Magpies to keep you entertained. Check the shady patches under the larger trees, as well as their lower branches, for birds such as Cirl Bunting and Red-legged Partridge.

Broad river valleys with sandy soils are good places to watch Bee-eaters; they nest in the low sandy ridges and banks that were eroded when the rivers were in spate during the winter rains. A bit of watching will soon reveal the favoured perches of these colourful birds giving you a chance of a decent photo. Black Storks and Grey Herons will often be present as will another colourful bird, the Kingfisher.

Large reservoirs can also be worth a visit this month to see Little Terns and Collared Pratincoles that both breed on the islands that are formed as the water levels drop. In the shallows, Black-winged Stilts with young will noisily protest every time a Black Kite drifts by.

Small bird to see: The Melodious Warbler can be found in scrubby habitat and woodland throughout the region. Not as shy as some, it can still be a bit tricky as it flits through the interior of the trees and bushes. A bit of time put in though is usually rewarded with the bird sitting up and singing from the top of a tree or exposed branch, the subtle yellow underparts showing well in the sunlight.

Potential Mega: Large numbers of Griffon Vultures are often spotted on the ground after feeding at a carcass or rubbish tip. There can sometimes be well over one hundred birds together; whilst this is a spectacle in itself, it is well worth meticulously checking the Griffons, as individual immature Rüppell's Vulture have started to appear with their larger cousins. Coming from Africa, one or two of these birds usually appear in southern Spain every year and recently they have also appeared in

Extremadura. Look for a bird that is noticeably smaller than the others with obviously darker wings and back. They can look a bit like a dirty undernourished version of the Griffon!

June Diary Excerpts:

...after a bit of searching I spotted a pair of White-rumped Swift flying around. A Black Vulture drifted by joining the numerous Griffons in the air and then I spotted a Spanish Imperial Eagle very high...

...there were a couple of Cirl Bunting about, a Great Spotted Woodpecker and down by the river we had some Thekla Lark. A Booted Eagle, this time a dark bird, flew...

...lots of Black Kite, a Common Buzzard, a Red Kite, several Griffon Vultures, one Black Vulture, a pale phase Booted Eagle, loads of White Stork, Bee-eaters and a Roller. Not bad for a drive to the supermarket...

...a group of 10 Collared Pratincole flying over the water and several Little Terns feeding. Around the edges there were White Stork, Little Egret, several Cattle Egret, a Grey Heron, some Black-winged Stilt, numerous White Wagtail...

...a few Ortolan Bunting singing, numerous Dunnock and Wren. Good views of Spanish Ibex on the rocky slopes higher up, whilst Rock Thrush and Rock Bunting...

...good views of a Melodious Warbler and down by the stream there was a 'riot' of Nightingale and Golden Oriole song – lovely. Overhead, amongst the constant Griffons, there were two Black Vultures and a Bonelli's Eagle...

...scanning from the ridge I soon found three Great Bustard, perhaps they were cashing in on the abundance of grasshoppers? A group of 34 White Stork definitely were! Three Pin-tailed Sandgrouse flew by...

July

Migrants Present

Purple Heron; Black Stork; Spoonbill; Honey Buzzard; Black Kite; Egyptian Vulture; Short-toed Eagle; Montagu's Harrier; Booted Eagle; Lesser Kestrel; Hobby; Collared Pratincole; Gull-billed Tern; Little Tern; Turtle Dove; Scops Owl; Common Nightjar; Red-necked Nightjar; Alpine Swift; Common Swift; Pallid Swift; White-rumped Swift; Bee-eater; Short-toed Lark; Sand Martin; Barn Swallow; Red-rumped Swallow; House Martin; Rufous Bush Robin; Nightingale; Redstart; Black-eared Wheatear; Rock Thrush; Savi's Warbler; Reed Warbler; Great Reed Warbler; Melodious Warbler; Western Orphean Warbler; Whitethroat; Spectacled Warbler; Subalpine Warbler; Bonelli's Warbler; Spotted Flycatcher; Golden Oriole; Red-backed Shrike; Woodchat Shrike; Ortolan Bunting. (46)

Migrants Arriving

Lapwing; Green Sandpiper; Common Sandpiper; Sedge Warbler. (4)

Migrants Departing

Common Quail; Great Spotted Cuckoo; Common Cuckoo; Roller. (4)

On Passage

None

Total Potential Species Including Residents: 159

July is hot with temperatures in the high thirties Celsius. It is fairly stable bird wise with just four birds departing and four birds arriving. The Rollers go early as do the two Cuckoos. Black Kites, their numbers swelled by birds from further north, are everywhere this month as they prepare to head south in August.

This is a good month to head up to the hills and mountains of northern Cáceres where the air is a bit cooler and fresher. Deciduous Oak woodlands replace the evergreens of the dehesa and a different bird life can be found. Western Bonelli's Warbler can be abundant in the Oaks, whilst out on the scrub, Spectacled Warbler can be found. Hobby and Honey Buzzard both patrol the skies of the wooded valleys, whilst high up on the passes into the neighbouring provinces, birds such as Rock Thrush, Ortolan Bunting and Red-backed Shrike can be found. A walk through the woods can find Short-toed Treecreepers, Spotted Flycatchers and, in the Pines, Coal Tit and Great Spotted Woodpecker.

Broken open country with plenty of rocks is a good place to see the Black-eared Wheatear, the males paler parts almost bleached white by the sun. Short-toed Eagles, usually accompanied by their solitary youngster, spend a lot of time in this habitat this month hunting snakes to try and satisfy their hungry offspring, which often advertises its presence with constant beg calling.

Many of the rivers are reduced to a string of pools as the heat dries up the shallower sections. These pools can hold concentrations of amphibians and fish which attract Grey and Purple Herons, Kingfishers and the occasional Cormorant. The edges of the larger pools are home to White Wagtails and Green Sandpipers, whilst a whole host of small birds will drop down to drink on a regular basis.

Shallow reservoirs on the edges of towns and villages can hold large concentrations of Common Coot, Great Crested Grebe and Little Grebe. Dozens of Black-winged Stilt and Common Sandpiper are also likely to be present.

Small bird to see: In the Pine forests of the hills and mountains, the Crested Tit can be found fairly easily. The small Tit can be unobtrusive but its distinctive trill like call often draws your attention to it.

Potential Mega: Not content with Pallid, Common, Alpine and White-rumped Swift? Then keep an eye out for the Little Swift. This birds population is expanding northwards in to Europe from Africa and the bird is no longer considered as an official rarity in Spain, where it breeds in Andalucia. However it is definitely a mega in Extremadura with a couple of sightings of individuals in the last few years, is this the beginning of a colonisation? Look for its small House Martin like shape which helps to distinguish from the forked tailed White-rumped Swift.

July Diary Excerpts:

...on arrival we could see one of the juvenile Golden Eagles sat near the nest in the shade. Meanwhile on the reservoir edge there were at least eight Green Sandpiper feeding...

...had a Raven and lovely views of a Black Stork before getting fantastic views of a Short-toed Eagle that was sat majestically on a roadside telegraph pole...

...heard more Azure-winged Magpies giving warning calls and soon spotted the reason – a Red Fox cub standing in the shade of one of the Oaks...

...as we dropped into the valley we had three Black-eared Wheatears and several Corn Bunting whilst overhead a couple of Black Kites drifted past. Higher still were a few Griffon Vultures and a Black Vulture...

...a couple of dozen Spanish Sparrows were drinking and bathing at the waters edge whilst an Iberian Grey Shrike looked on. As we walked further we flushed a Purple Heron from the reeds...

...there were three Short-toed Eagles drifting over us, there was a fair bit of calling from them and one of them had half a snake hanging out of its bill...

...several White Storks and a couple of Grey Herons were patrolling the edges, out on the water there were at least 100 Coot, dozens of Great Crested Grebe as well as Little Grebe...

Great Crested Grebe

August

Migrants Present

Purple Heron; Black Stork; Spoonbill; Honey Buzzard; Egyptian Vulture; Short-toed Eagle; Montagu's Harrier; Booted Eagle; Lesser Kestrel; Hobby; Collared Pratincole; Lapwing; Green Sandpiper; Common Sandpiper; Turtle Dove; Scops Owl; Common Nightjar; Red-necked Nightjar; Alpine Swift; Pallid Swift; White-rumped Swift; Bee-eater; Short-toed Lark; Sand Martin; Barn Swallow; Red-rumped Swallow; House Martin; Nightingale; Redstart; Black-eared Wheatear; Rock Thrush; Savi's Warbler; Sedge Warbler; Reed Warbler; Great Reed Warbler; Melodious Warbler; Whitethroat; Spectacled Warbler; Subalpine Warbler; Bonelli's Warbler; Spotted Flycatcher; Golden Oriole; Woodchat Shrike; Ortolan Bunting. (44)

Migrants Arriving

Teal; Shoveler; Pochard; Osprey; Ringed Plover; Little Stint; Curlew Sandpiper; Dunlin; Snipe; Spotted Redshank; Redshank; Greenshank; Wood Sandpiper; Tree Pipit; Yellow Wagtail; Northern Wheatear; Garden Warbler; Willow Warbler; Pied Flycatcher. (19)

Migrants Departing

Black Kite; Gull-billed Tern; Little Tern; Common Swift; Rufous Bush Robin; Western Orphean Warbler; Red-backed Shrike. (7)

On Passage

None

Total Potential Species Including Residents: 175

August is hot, sometimes even touching 40°, but, despite the heat, this is a good month for birds arriving, with 19 species passing through and stopping for several weeks. Seven species depart, including the Black Kite, abundant at the very beginning of the month they are all gone by the end of it.

This is good month to head for the many reservoirs in the region to catch some of the arrivals as they feed up after their long journey. Scan the skies and any waterside perch points such as trees and pylons for Ospreys, increasingly Extremadura is becoming a regular stopping off point for these majestic fish hunters as they fly south from their breeding grounds. Even the smaller reservoirs on the edges of villages and towns are used, especially those that are stocked with fish. Keep an eye out on the water's edge for Yellow Wagtails that can arrive in large numbers as the month wears on, several different races can be seen. Several waders can be found this month too, particularly late in the evening, as they look for somewhere to roost, any islands created by falling water levels are well worth a good scan.

Rocky ridges should also be visited, other than the Black Kite, all of the breeding raptors are present and, with their young out of the nest, can often be found perched up on the rocks. Listen out for the youngsters begging calls as these can be a good way to find an otherwise unseen bird. Late in the afternoon the skies around these ridges can be filled with large parties of Alpine Swift screaming low overhead as you watch. Keep an eye out for their much smaller cousin, the White Rumped Swift, as this too haunts the same areas.

Short turfed fields with stone walls surrounding them are worth a look for Northern Wheatear as it stops off for an extended stay on its return journey to its wintering grounds.

Small bird to see: The Thekla Lark is a bird that can cause confusion, it closely resembles the more abundant Crested Lark, but with care it can be told apart. Thekla prefer sloping, broken country (although can be found elsewhere), try and get good views of the head, looking in particular at the shorter more typical bill shape and less spiky crest of the Thekla Lark. Don't believe the books that tell you that Thekla Larks perch in bushes and Crested Larks don't, this is just not true. Crested Larks will perch in bushes and on gates, just as Thekla Larks do. Thekla Larks tend to look plumper than Crested but the bill and crest are the best identifying features to look for.

Thekla Lark, note small bill and more fan like, than spiky crest

Potential Mega: The Dotterel is a small wader that occasionally breeds in very low numbers elsewhere in Spain. After breeding, it passes through central Spain on the journey south and, in small numbers, can be found in Extremadura when doing so. Usually found in open habitats like steppe, it doesn't stop for long and records are scarce.

August Diary Excerpts:

...Short-toed Eagle fly along the ridge then briefly drop the other side, when it reappeared I spotted an adult Spanish Imperial Eagle some way above, it was quite a way off but the distinctive shape and white on the wing edges were easily visible...

...saw some more Alpine Swifts through the rocks and then a smaller Swift caught my eye but quickly vanished. It appeared again and very briefly I saw a white rump as it banked and vanished again. It came back into view and flew right by us showing its white rump and the distinctive white throat/chin — White-rumped Swift!...

...great views of an Egyptian Vulture flying low above us, a Black Stork flew by too, the light bringing out the iridescence...

...whilst watching the Red Deer a Crested Lark suddenly took flight and into the binoculars came a dark phase Booted Eagle that was obviously having a 'pop' at it...

...a male Blue Rock Thrush posed nicely for us and we were about to leave when a female Sparrowhawk appeared...

...a group of the Spanish race of Long-tailed Tits appeared and came in very close followed by an obliging Crested Tit. Lower down a male Subalpine Warbler was skulking...

...in the heat I looked across the reservoir and saw an Osprey flying low above the water heading straight towards me...

Male Blue Rock Thrush

September

Migrants Present

Teal; Shoveler; Pochard; Black Stork; Spoonbill; Booted Eagle; Osprey; Ringed Plover; Lapwing; Little Stint; Curlew Sandpiper; Dunlin; Snipe; Spotted Redshank; Greenshank; Green Sandpiper; Wood Sandpiper; Common Sandpiper; Alpine Swift; Pallid Swift; White-rumped Swift; Red-rumped Swallow; House Martin; Tree Pipit; Yellow Wagtail; Redstart; Northern Wheatear; Garden Warbler; Whitethroat; Subalpine Warbler; Willow Warbler; Spotted Flycatcher; Pied Flycatcher; Ortolan Bunting. (34)

Migrants Arriving

Pintail; Black-necked Grebe; Skylark; Tawny Pipit; Meadow Pipit; Whinchat; Chiffchaff; Firecrest. (8)

Migrants Departing

Purple Heron; Honey Buzzard; Egyptian Vulture; Short-toed Eagle; Montagu's Harrier; Lesser Kestrel; Hobby; Collared Pratincole; Redshank; Turtle Dove; Scops Owl; Common Nightjar; Red-necked Nightjar; Bee-eater; Short-toed Lark; Sand Martin; Barn Swallow; Nightingale; Black-eared Wheatear; Rock Thrush; Savi's Warbler; Sedge Warbler; Reed Warbler; Great Reed Warbler; Melodious Warbler; Spectacled Warbler; Bonelli's Warbler; Golden Oriole; Woodchat Shrike. (29)

On Passage

Gargany (1)

Total Potential Species Including Residents: 177

September is a much fresher month than the previous two, it is still warm but there is an almost spring like feel to it, with many of the resident passerines singing again. A large number of summer migrants depart this month, with only a handful arriving.

This is a good month to head into the dehesa, small birds abound, Willow Warblers are very numerous but it is the Pied Flycatchers that are the most abundant. The resident smaller birds are also conspicuous, singing loudly and seemingly enjoying the fresher weather now that the heat of summer is over. Parties of Azure-winged Magpie will be feeding throughout the trees and on the turf below, Hoopoes can also be easily found. All of this small bird activity doesn't go unnoticed and Booted Eagles can often be seen hunting this habitat at this time of year.

Like last month, the reservoirs are good places to visit in September, the Ospreys are still present and the waders really begin to form large groups. For the latter, the shallower, smaller reservoirs on the edges of towns and villages can be particularly rewarding.

Black-winged Stilt

Whilst at the reservoirs on the edges of the towns and villages, check out also the narrow streets that are criss-crossed with wires, those that are in the sun will be covered with hundreds of House Martins as they flock together prior to their departure next month. Spotless Starlings also form noisy groups in the towns where they are often less wary, enabling photo opportunities.

Small bird to see: Rock Sparrows can be easily overlooked, but with their restricted European distribution they are a bird to be searched for. In September the best places to look are the stock ponds in amongst the dehesa. Many birds will be taking advantage of this water supply, but keep your eye out for these birds with their boldly striped heads. The white tips to the tail feathers can often catch your eye in the light as they fly in towards the pond.

Potential Mega: The Cream-coloured Courser is a semi desert inhabiting species found across north Africa. Extremadura has one record of this bird from September 2011 but with the close proximity of the African population and plenty of arid steppe there is certainly potential for more.

September Diary Excerpts:

...in the Cork Oaks, along with the abundant Willow Warblers and Pied Flycatchers, were several Chaffinch, Blue Tit, a Nuthatch, a couple of Cirl Bunting, the odd Jay, several noisy Azure-wings and a Hoopoe...

...good views of a juvenile Golden Eagle as it took off and gained height, the white in the tail and the wings reflecting the low sunlight. As I continued walking I

heard a noise to my right and had a brief view of a Beech Marten scurrying away...

...there were ten Little Egrets in a loose group with the Black Stork stood still in amongst them. Several Greenshank were dashing around, in between them and whilst watching these, I noticed a Yellow Wagtail busily feeding a few yards from me...

...suddenly on our left a Griffon Vulture flew low above the trees, right behind it a female Spanish Imperial in hot pursuit, the white feathers on her shoulders really standing out against her dark plumage...

...I counted a total of 62 Black-winged Stilt in a large loose group. In with them were 3 Spotted Redshank, a few Greenshank, some Common Sandpipers and 4 Little Ringed Plovers...

...an Iberian Grey Shrike and its young being noisy, whilst off in the distance a Griffon Vulture and a Raven flew by. A small bird caught my eye — a Whinchat passing through...

...the resident Ravens were about and calling noisily as a pair of higher up Bonelli's Eagle flew past. A Wild Boar was trotting along the far bank...

October

Migrants Present

Teal; Pintail; Shoveler; Pochard; Black-necked Grebe; Lapwing; Dunlin; Snipe; Greenshank; Green Sandpiper; Common Sandpiper; Skylark; Meadow Pipit; Chiffchaff; Firecrest; Pied Flycatcher. (16)

Migrants Arriving

Greylag Goose; Wigeon; Tufted Duck; Hen Harrier; Merlin; Common Crane; Stock Dove; Water Pipit; Bluethroat; Song Thrush; Common Starling; Siskin; Bullfinch. (13)

Migrants Departing

Black Stork; Spoonbill; Booted Eagle; Osprey; Ringed Plover; Little Stint; Curlew Sandpiper; Spotted Redshank; Wood Sandpiper; Alpine Swift; Pallid Swift; White-rumped Swift; Red-rumped Swallow; House Martin; Tawny Pipit; Tree Pipit; Yellow Wagtail; Redstart; Whinchat; Northern Wheatear; Garden Warbler; Whitethroat; Subalpine Warbler; Willow Warbler; Spotted Flycatcher; Ortolan Bunting. (26)

On Passage

None

Total Potential Species Including Residents: 160

October is the beginning of autumn weather wise, the temperatures start to drop at night, especially with clear skies and often the first significant rains since March fall. Virtually all of the remaining summer migrants depart this month, but they are replaced with several wintering ones, including one of the stars of Extremadura's avifauna, the Common Crane.

This is a good month to explore around the small fields and scrubby areas that are often found around villages. Meadow Pipits start arriving this month and before long form very large flocks. These in turn attract Sparrowhawks, although there is a small resident population of this raptor in Extremadura they are seldom seen, but in the winter, northern birds following the migrating small birds can be seen frequently, especially where they can exploit the cover found around villages etc.

It is also a good month to head out on to the plains where yet more Meadow Pipits can be found, they are joined by Common Starling who can be seen intermingling with the large flocks of Spotless Starlings that forage this habitat at this time of year. The month also sees the arrival of the magnificent Hen Harrier and the small, but dashing Merlin, both of which will be seeking to exploit the large numbers of small birds that are congregating on the open plains.

The reservoirs are still worth a look as a few Ospreys are beginning to stay longer and longer with a few now over wintering. Wigeon and Tufted Duck start arriving in numbers and there will still be several wader species to see as well.

Overhead and towards the end of the month large 'V' formations of Crane and Greylag Goose can be seen as they head into the region for the winter.

Small bird to see: Although relatively common in parts of Extremadura, the Cirl Bunting can be difficult to find. At this time of year however, they form small parties and will frequent dehesa habitat, still unobtrusive in their habits, this is a good month for seeing these birds.

Potential Mega: The Pectoral Sandpiper is a North American wader that is an annual vagrant to western Europe. There are ten records for Extremadura and almost all of them involve individual juvenile birds passing through in late September and October.

Wigeon start to arrive in number this month and can be seen along with Teal in large numbers

October Diary Excerpts:

...first stop was to look at a Penduline Tits nest I found back in June, an amazing structure and we didn't have to wait long to see its maker...

...had an Egyptian Vulture soaring over the valley which is a good late sighting and later on, a Booted Eagle, again a late sighting...

...I saw the first group of a couple of dozen Meadow Pipits, by the time I had got to the reservoir I had seen loads. You know winters on its way when they arrive...

...the usual Blackbird, Serin, and Sardinian Warbler as well as a group of Linnet and Goldfinch lined the track edges as a couple of Griffon Vultures flew by effortlessly...

...a Golden Eagle, a long way off, in full adult plumage. A bit further down there were two Black Vultures in flight and by the bridge there were several Griffons and a Common Kestrel as well as numerous Crag Martins...

...there were 27 Griffon Vultures and 3 Black Vultures circling in the thermal, a Common Buzzard, dwarfed by the huge vultures, joined them and right at the top of the stack the distinctive 'T' of a Sparrowhawk...

...in the scrub with the Azure-winged Magpies were Blackcap, Robin, loads of Chiffchaff, Sardinian Warbler and a showy Dartford...

November

Migrants Present

Greylag Goose; Wigeon; Teal; Pintail; Shoveler; Pochard; Tufted Duck; Black-necked Grebe; Hen Harrier; Merlin; Common Crane; Lapwing; Dunlin; Snipe; Greenshank; Green Sandpiper; Stock Dove; Skylark; Meadow Pipit; Water Pipit; Bluethroat; Song Thrush; Chiffchaff; Firecrest; Common Starling; Siskin; Bullfinch. (27)

Migrants Arriving

Golden Plover; Curlew; Fieldfare; Redwing; Goldcrest; Brambling; Reed Bunting. (7)

Migrants Departing

Common Sandpiper; Pied Flycatcher. (2)

On Passage

None

Total Potential Species Including Residents: 141

November is a much colder month than October and the rain can be more frequent. The last wintering migrants arrive whilst the last of the prolonged late summer passage birds depart.

November is a good month to head to the rice growing areas, the Cranes have arrived and will be everywhere, as will Greylag Goose and White Storks. Keep an eye out for smaller birds too, with Reed Bunting and Bluethroat both wintering in this habitat, sometimes in large numbers. Black Shouldered Kites become more obvious at this time of year and form small roosts, the rice fields can be good spots to see these birds as the light begins to fade.

It is also a good month to head out on to the plains, large numbers of Golden Plover will have joined the Starlings and Lapwing and the Great Bustards can form very large groups at this time. The flocks of lark and pipits usually mean that a Hen Harrier isn't that far away and as these glide over the land they can suddenly put up flocks of Little Bustard that also form large groups at this time.

Steep sided river valleys can be good spots on sunny days as these are more likely to generate uplift than other areas, something that all raptors will readily exploit. Birds like Black Wheatear can also be found in this habitat and their busy feeding behaviour can be quite noticeable in the colder weather.

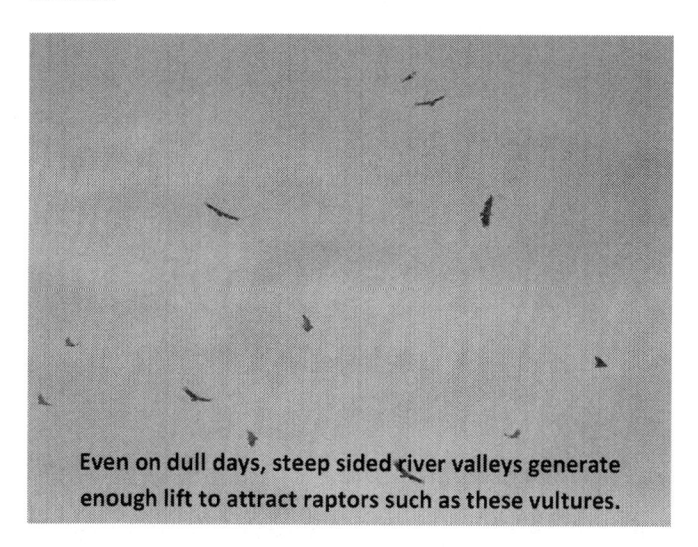

Even on dull days, steep sided river valleys generate enough lift to attract raptors such as these vultures.

Small bird to see: Extremadura abounds with Larks, most are resident, but the Skylark is primarily a winter visitor to the majority of Extremadura. They can form large flocks in the winter and are found in agricultural areas, steppe and dehesa.

Potential Mega: With over 100,000 Common Cranes arriving in the region for the winter there is potential for a mega to turn up in amongst them. The Sandhill Crane is a North American species but, in recent years, individual birds have turned up in the European population. An individual Sandhill Crane was recorded in Extremadura in November 2011, spotting it among 100,000 other Cranes though could be difficult!

November Diary Excerpts:

...we had eight Pin-tailed Sandgrouse take off close to us giving really good views before we then picked up on five Black-bellied Sandgrouse in flight further off...

...a group of 32 Crane in flight, whilst nearer to me a Red Kite drifted along. A female Merlin flew in from behind me and obliging perched at the top of a nearby tree...

...we had great views of a male Black Wheatear and a group of four Thekla Larks as well as Serin and lots of Goldfinch. In the sky there were the usual Griffon Vultures, a couple of Red Kite and a Sparrowhawk...

...brilliant views of a Little Owl enabling yet more photo opportunities. We saw lots of Lapwing and then, perched together on a telegraph pole, a pair of Bonelli's Eagle...

...lots of Green Sandpiper, a largish group of Dunlin, a few Common Sandpiper, a couple of Black-winged Stilt, Greenshank, a Ringed Plover, Kingfisher, lots of White Wagtails and a Water Pipit. Out on the water were loads of Coot, Great Crested Grebe and Mallard as well as a few Gadwall, lots of Tufted Duck, lots of Little Grebe and a few Black-necked Grebe...

...both the male and female Spanish Imperial Eagles flew straight over us before circling, gaining height and drifting off...

...I spotted one, then two Great Bustard striding purposefully along. I put the clients on to them and then scanned in the direction the two were headed, I couldn't believe my own eyes when another 41 Great Bustards came into view...

December

Migrants Present

Greylag Goose; Wigeon; Teal; Pintail; Shoveler; Pochard; Tufted Duck; Black-necked Grebe; Hen Harrier; Merlin; Common Crane; Golden Plover; Lapwing; Dunlin; Snipe; Curlew; Greenshank; Green Sandpiper; Stock Dove; Skylark; Meadow Pipit; Water Pipit; Bluethroat; Fieldfare; Song Thrush; Redwing; Chiffchaff; Goldcrest; Firecrest; Common Starling; Brambling; Siskin; Bullfinch; Reed Bunting. (34)

Migrants Arriving

None

Migrants Departing

None

On Passage

None

Total Potential Species Including Residents: 139

December can often be dryer than the proceeding two months, but with clear skies it can also get down to freezing on many nights. It is a very stable month in terms of bird movements with no migrants either arriving or departing.

This is a good month to head out on to the steppe, particularly in the late afternoon as the low sun can really pick out the markings of many of the steppe species. Both species of

Sandgrouse will often fly towards the end of the day and when seen in this light you can really appreciate the beauty of their plumage. Both Bustards are still in large groups and the Calandra Lark have also formed big flocks.

At the beginning of the day, you can get great views of birds trying to get the first rays of sunshine. Pylons are favourite places, with flocks of Spotless Starlings competing with Red Kites and Common Buzzard for the best spots.

Scrub and dehesa areas are also good places to visit this month, Woodlark and Cirl Bunting are just two species that are easier to see at this time of year. Away from the dehesa, but still in amongst trees, particularly Olive and Narrow Leaved Ash, you can find the Hawfinch, look for the distinctive wing flash as they fly and listen for their harsh 'tix' call.

Areas looking over dehesa can also be very productive as huge flocks of Woodpigeon can be found as they take advantage of the acorn crop. Flocks of several thousand birds can be seen and these often attract the attention of the resident Eagles, especially Bonelli's and also Peregrine Falcons.

Small bird to see: In the winter the Firecrest can be found in virtually all of Extremadura other than the open, treeless habitats such as steppe. Whilst favouring conifers it is also found in dehesa and even in amenity trees in urban parks. This small, busy little bird is always a good bird to find.

Potential Mega: The North American Lesser Yellowlegs is an annual vagrant to western Europe but it is still a very rare visitor to Extremadura with only three records. However, in the last two years a solitary bird has been recorded from December through to January at various wetland sites in the region, so they are definitely one to keep an eye out for.

Flocks of 10,000 plus Woodpigeon can be seen, especially in the Sierra de San Pedro. These huge flocks attract Raptors from all around.

December Diary Excerpts:

...had a Black-winged Kite hovering alongside the road, really showing well. Several Marsh Harriers as you would expect, lots of Grey Herons and a Great Egret which...

...several glimpses of Hawfinch before one finally sat and gave good views. Lots of Azure-winged Magpies, Serin, Blue and Great Tits as well as Hoopoe, Blackbird, Song Thrush, Chaffinch and Blackcap...

...lots of Griffon Vultures and Cranes overhead. On the plains the Calandra Larks have formed large flocks and these and Corn Bunting were abundant. Several Golden Plover and Lapwing about as well as nice views of two male Hen Harriers. Five Little Bustards flew over us...

...first bird we saw on getting out of the car was a lovely low Golden Eagle that showed brilliantly as it flew through the valley...

...a solitary Red Kite and yet another group of four Crane. Spotted a group of five Woodlark on the edge of the track whilst in the dehesa there were a flock of Azure-winged Magpies joined by several Spotless Starlings, a Cirl Bunting and a party of Long-tailed Tits...

...in perfect light we saw a group of 29 Great Bustard very close, a flock of 34 Little Bustard, 29 Pin-tailed Sandgrouse in flight and in total 40 Black-bellied Sandgrouse, five of which flew...

...several thousand Crane both on the ground and overhead. There were also several hundred Greylag Geese on the wet meadows...

Part 2

-The habitats, birding areas and the star species of Extremadura

Main Habitats of Extremadura

Extremadura has a wealth of very different habitats, from wild high mountain tops to intensively farmed lowland arable areas. Sometimes the habitat is extensive, covering many square miles and at other times it is a just small pocket covering a few hundred metres. The greatest diversity is found in the province of Cáceres, but Badajoz, whilst not as diverse, is home to some valuable habitat in its own right, including some of the largest expanses of steppe to be found in the region.

Six main habitats are covered here; the first of which forms what is arguably Extremadura's most iconic landscape.

Dehesa:

Endless Dehesa in the Sierra de San Pedro, home to the largest number of Spanish Imperial Eagle in Extremadura

Although in places originating from what would have been natural woodland cover, the open, almost parkland type woodland of Evergreen and Cork Oak dehesa that covers large areas of the region is entirely a man made habitat. Strictly speaking, dehesa is farmland that is planted with trees that are allowed to mature, forming an open woodland like habitat. The land is farmed underneath the trees, mainly for grazing but also, sometimes, for growing cereal crops. The trees are pruned to produce a spreading canopy of branches that act as cover to protect the soils, the grass or crops and the animals from the punishing summer sun as well as producing a crop themselves. The Evergreen Oaks produce large sweet acorns (Bellota in Spanish) which are used to fatten the pigs that make the legendary Iberico Ham that the region is justly famous for. The Cork Oaks have their outer bark harvested every 10 or so years producing cork for use in flooring, insulation and, of course, wine making. It might not be a natural habitat, but this combination of trees and open space below them is host to a wonderful array of wildlife.

The grassland beneath the trees can be alive with colour in the spring as the wild flowers burst into life. Sometimes a kaleidoscope of colours can be seen, at other times just one colour dominates. This floral display is very dependent on how much rain has fallen in late winter and early spring, but if the rains haven't failed, the sight is truly breathtaking, with flowers forming carpets of colour underneath the dark green branches of both of the non deciduous Oaks.

Lavender carpeting the dehesa floor

Although dehesa normally has farmed land beneath it, in some areas, particularly hilly areas, this has been replaced by scrub adding to the wildlife value of the habitat. Other than the specialist steppe and wetland species virtually all of Extremadura's birds can be found in the dehesa. Perhaps the most symbolic bird of this habitat is the Spanish Imperial Eagle. This eagle was once widely found across the Iberian Peninsula and even into Morocco on the other side of the Gibraltar Straits. Sadly, through habitat loss, illegal persecution and a severe decline in its natural prey item (the rabbit), this majestic raptor was reduced to just a handful of isolated populations. Thankfully, due to strident conservation efforts, the population is now much stronger and is now expanding from these areas to re-colonise its former range.

In 2012 the global population of this bird was 380 pairs (only 10 of these were not in Spain), of these, 53 pairs, or 14%, bred, in Extremadura. Within Extremadura, the area with the most pairs is the Sierra de San Pedro ZEPA (a designation similar to the British SSSI). Unlike its relation the Golden Eagle, Spanish

Imperials prefer to nest in trees, the large pruned branches of the dehesa oaks are ideal for supporting their large nests.

> **BIRDING TIP!**
> *If it rains whilst you are out birding in the dehesa find a spot with a good vantage point overlooking the trees and wait for the rain to stop. Most birds of prey enjoy the warmth of the sun on them after rain has past and the Spanish Imperial is no exception. They can be the first bird in the sky once the sun has re-emerged, energetically flying around to dry their plumage off. Rain can sometimes be helpful!*

Another star of this habitat is the beautiful Azure-winged Magpie. Highly gregarious you won't see just one on its own, but they can be wary, with only a few showing themselves at any one time. They are opportunistic feeders taking advantage of anything that is on offer, in the dehesa they primarily feed on insects, often hopping along the ground in pursuit of them. They are curious birds and, if used to people, will sometimes come in very close. They are found throughout most of the region in habitats where there are at least some trees, but it is the dehesa that is the natural home of this colourful bird.

Adding to the colour, and creating the backing track, is the Hoopoe, like the Azure-wing it can be found in many different habitats but it is most at home in amongst the oaks of the dehesa. Once a spring and summer visitor this unique bird can now be found the whole year through. Look for it probing the ground in the shadow of the trees as this is often where the best insect food is found.

In the winter the dehesa is home to yet another iconic species, the Crane. The majority of the European breeding population of this graceful bird winters in Extremadura, the last survey counted over 128,000 individuals! Also found in large numbers in the wetland areas, the dehesa is where many choose to feed, the month of February is the time when the Cranes are easiest to find amongst the trees as they feed continuously on the acorn crop fattening up for the long journey back to their breeding grounds.

Apart from the birds there are a wealth of insects in the dehesa, most of which seem to go to feed the birds! In the spring, Butterflies abound, whilst later on the large grasshoppers proliferate offering a high protein meal to birds as diverse as Azure-winged Magpie, White Stork and Black Kite. Mammals are present but typically difficult to see. The easiest to find is the Red Deer, many of the large estates actively encourage this species, and Wild Boar, for hunting purposes so both are relatively common. Whilst the Wild Boar is predominantly nocturnal, the Red Deer can be seen throughout the day, in the heat of the summer they can sometimes be found lying up in the shade of an oak, but it is the rut, beginning in September, when they are at their most obvious, the bellowing roars of the stags echoing around the landscape.

Red Deer, like this young stag can often be seen in amongst the dehesa

There are good areas of dehesa throughout the region. Three areas that offer particularly good examples are: Sierra de San Pedro (Badajoz/Cáceres); Campo Arañuelo (Cáceres) and the area between Monfragüe and Monroy (Cáceres).

Steppe/Plains:

The plains can seem endless and empty, but they are full of life

The vast open plains are yet another man made agricultural habitat that is home to a fantastic array of wildlife. Technically classified as psuedosteppe, the thin soils can only support extensive grazing systems for beef cattle and sheep. Where there is a bit more depth to the soil, cereal crops such as wheat can be grown, if it is a wet spring then hay can also be successfully harvested from this landscape. In the hot dry summer this is a very harsh landscape for the livestock to survive in, consequently Vultures are often seen scanning the area for carcasses and this habitat offers the best opportunity of seeing these large birds on the ground.

When a carcass is spotted, Black Vultures, Griffon Vultures and, in the spring and summer, Egyptian Vultures, drop in from all around. Sometimes well over a hundred birds can congregate at a dead animal; it has been estimated that from the first Griffon

Vulture arriving at an adult sheep carcass there will be nothing left within 45 minutes.

Two Black Vultures stood beside a sheep carcass on the Membrio/Brozas steppe

Vultures will gorge themselves full of food and have to let it begin to digest before they are able to fly off again. They can often be seen stood loafing about out in the open whilst they digest their meal.

As with the dehesa this habitat can be a riot of colour in the spring, but, without the shade of the trees to protect them, the flowers are quickly burnt off. Grassland butterflies predominate and Crickets and Grasshoppers are everywhere.

Egyptian Grasshoppers can be 8cms in length.

> **BIRDING TIP!**
> The plains may look flat and featureless but they are actually full of small undulations. The Great Bustard is a master at exploiting these dips and rises, ensuring that it keeps out of sight. When scanning an area, scan the same area from several vantage points to maximise your chances. The results can be surprising – I once scanned an area that I knew would hold Great Bustard. From two different spots I found nothing, but from the third I saw 43 of them!

There is no doubting which bird species is the star of this habitat, the Great Bustard is the must see bird of the plains. The Great Bustard is a large bird, it is the heaviest flying bird in the world, but its size doesn't mean that it is easy to see! These birds can be very wary and will actively avoid human activity, but, with patient scanning of the right habitat it shouldn't take you long to locate some of these magnificent birds.

April is a good month to see these birds display, the males exuberantly turning white to impress the females. In the winter they can form large groups of several dozen birds and are perhaps easier to see at this time than at other times of the year. But, whenever you go to Extremadura, Great Bustards can be found striding along these wonderful grasslands.

The Little Bustard is another must see bird of the plains, like the Great it is present all year round. In the winter they form large flocks, sometimes forming groups of over 200 birds. In the spring, the males perform their bizarre mating call, sounding like someone blowing a raspberry, this call carries a long way across the grassland. It will sound deceptively close but is actually unlikely to be within 100m of you, so make sure you scan further afield than your ears are telling you to. Look out for the plumped up black neck feathers of the male as he makes his call, the bird usually does so from a slight rise or low lying rocks but with the long grass of spring he can be tricky to locate.

Pin-tailed and Black-bellied Sandgrouse can also be found on the plains. These beautifully marked birds can be spotted on the ground through patient scanning but are normally picked up in flight. Whilst flying, these birds make very distinctive calls, listening out for these can be key to seeing these otherwise elusive species. Black-bellied Sandgrouse has a rolling, bubbling sort of call whilst the Pin-tailed has a slurring call that reminds me of a higher pitched Raven's cronk. Listening to these calls on the internet before your visit is a good way of getting to know what to listen out for.

With a chunky bill and black neck markings, the Calandra Lark is a distinctive bird.

The Calandra Lark is another typical bird of the plains, these chunky larks with their distinctive white bordered dark underwings, fill the air with song in the spring. Less obvious though are the Short-toed Lark and Tawny Pipit, but both can be found, the former in good numbers. Look along the edges of the many dusty tracks or in areas where the trampling of livestock has left bare areas of dried mud for your best chance of spotting these two easily missed birds.

Another bird associated with this habitat is the stunningly coloured Roller. Sadly, these birds are no longer as common as they once were but, thanks to the provision of nest boxes, there are areas where they still are numerous. Search for these birds where you find large numbers of nest boxes attached to telegraph posts and pylon lines that run alongside the roads that cross the plains. Other species such as Common Kestrel, Spotless Starling, Jackdaw and Little Owl all use these boxes but they are intended for Rollers.

A stunning pair of Rollers at their nest box on the Trujillo/Cáceres Plains.

In the winter the plains abound with Lapwing and huge numbers of wintering Meadow Pipit and Skylark. These birds, along with large numbers of Golden Plover and Spotless Starlings can form massive flocks providing a real spectacle. Check the Starlings to spot wintering Common Starlings that join their Spotless cousins from October onwards. These large aggregations of small birds don't go unnoticed, wintering Hen Harriers and Merlins can both be found hunting the plains at this time of year.

Mammals can also be seen on the plains, but are usually wary in such open landscapes. Red Deer and Red Fox can both be found, but the mammal most frequently seen is the Iberian Hare. Like its relation the Brown Hare, which can be found in the rest of Europe, this is a mammal that will sit very tight relying on its colouring to help it blend in to the vegetation.

The Iberian Hare, sat very still in the hope that you can't see it! A common mammal of the plains.

There are good examples of plains throughout the region. The largest is La Serena in Badajoz province. The network of steppe between Trujillo and Cáceres and the steppe between Membrio and Brozas, both in Cáceres province, are well worth exploring and are perhaps easier to view than the large La Serena.

Mountains

Extremadura is not known as an area of mountains, but in the north of Cáceres province, various off shoots of the chain of mountains that run across central Spain can be found. They provide a completely different habitat to anywhere else in the region.

The western end of the massive Sierra de Gredos mountain range runs into Extremadura in its north eastern corner, although not as high as the rest of the range, it is still over 2,200m in height. Running on west of this, and forming the boundary with Salamanca province to the north, is the beautiful Sierra de Gata, itself attaining heights of over 1500m.

The Sierra de Gredos, here in the neighbouring Avila province, extends into north eastern Cáceres.

Above the tree line, the terrain is covered in low vegetation dominated by species of Broom recalling the moorlands of Britain. Below this, steep wooded valleys of Pyrenean Oak and conifer provide a different sort of woodland to the more typical dehesa of the lower areas.

Of the many birds that can be found in this habitat it is perhaps the Honey Buzzard that is the star. This spring and summer migrant first appears in the month of April and can be found in many places in the Sierra de Gata and the slopes of the Gredos, particularly on the Valle de Jerte side.

> **BIRDING TIP!**
> On a bright sunny April/May morning find a viewpoint that overlooks the wooded slopes and wait for the thermals to start to rise. Honey Buzzards have a reputation for being difficult to identify, but during their wonderful butterfly like display flight they are unmistakeable! As the thermals start to rise off the warm slopes the birds take to their air circling and clapping their wings over their back. A great chance to get to know this sometimes difficult bird.

Up above the treeline, in the broom dominated scrub, smaller birds such as Northern Wheatear and Dunnock abound, but it is the Bluethroat that is the must see bird in this terrain. It is not hard to be find, sitting high in the vegetation and singing away on sunny spring days. Another bird that attracts attention to itself through it's voice is the Spectacled Warbler, listen out for the repeated whistled beginning to their song.

The Pyrenean Oak woods are good places to find the small Western Bonelli's Warbler as well as some of the small Extremaduran breeding population of Pied Flycatcher. Crested Tits can be found in the conifer woodlands all year around whilst in the spring and summer you may be lucky to see Hobby which has a small breeding population in Extremadura but is locally common in areas such as the Sierra de Gata.

There are many mammals to be found in the mountains, but they can be typically secretive. Roe Deer join the Red Deer and Wild Boar are also common in the wooded slopes but it is out on the tops of the mountains that the habitats star mammal can be found.

Spreading out from its nucleus in the Sierra de Gredos the Spanish Ibex can now be found throughout the Sierra de Gata as well. These sure footed wild goats make a mockery of the

A male Spanish Ibex in the Sierra de Gredos

rough, steep terrain and can often be spotted on the most inaccessible looking crags. They graze on the sparse vegetation and although they can be wary they will often permit close views if they are approached carefully.

There is controversy surrounding the presence of another mammal in the Sierra de Gata. The Wolf died out in Extremadura in the 1980s, but there is a thriving and expanding population of this iconic mammal on the Salamanca province side of the Sierra de Gata. The boundary between this province and Cáceres is just a line on the map; there is no physical boundary and therefore no reason why the Wolf won't venture over it. There have been numerous credible sightings of wolves in the north of Extremadura for many years but officially they are not present. If they were officially present then the government of Extremadura would be financially liable for any damage to livestock in the region. This may well be the reason for the Wolf not being *officially* found in Extremadura.

The Wolf, controversy surrounds the presence of this iconic mammal in the north of Cáceres province.

The Sierra de Gata is an extensive area and can be accessed from the many roads and tracks in the area. Vehicle access to the highest parts is simple as there are a number of roads that cross the Sierra from Cáceres province into Salamanca province, often providing stop off points allowing you to explore the treeless habitat. The wooded slopes can be accessed throughout but a good start is the area around San Martin de Trevejo, a particularly good location for Honey Buzzard.

The Extremaduran end of the mighty Sierra de Gredos range is not so accessible, although the minor road leading to the Puerto del Piornal takes you through very good habitat as does the road to the Puerto de Honduras. The steep wooded slopes can be accessed on foot from the Valle de Jerte, particularly from the La Garganta de los Infiernos reserve near the town of Jerte.

The wooded slopes of the Sierra de Gredos in Extremadura.

Cistus Scrub

Cistus scrub or el bosque mediterráneo as it is known in Spanish, is the dominant wild habitat of the region. Its importance to Extremadura's wildlife has been recognised by the wildlife organisations of the area and large areas have been painstakingly restored. The low shrubby structure of this habitat provides perfect nesting habitat for many small birds and abundant cover for small mammals, all of which mean that this is good habitat for spotting mammalian and avian predators.

Cistus scrub dominating an area of neglected dehesa. The combination of the scrub and the trees makes for great wildlife habitat

An abundance of flowering plants can be found in this habitat, the variety is enormous ensuring that anyone with an interest in botany will be kept very busy. The dominant plant though, and the one giving the habitat its English name, is the Jara Blanca or Common Gum Cistus. In the spring the white flowers transform the countryside, the whole habitat resounding to the hum of insects keen to exploit the plants nectar.

The beautiful flower of the Jara Blanca.

The habitat is often used by bee-keepers, placing their hives nearby to produce honey. The bees are, in turn, exploited by Bee-eaters that can often be found feeding in this habitat. The scrub is home to a number of small birds, Dartford warbler and Sardinian Warbler are very common, in areas where there are a few trees scattered through the habitat you may also find Subalpine Warbler and the rarer Western Orphean Warbler. The latter having a distinctive song of repeated notes recalling a Song Thrush.

Woodchat Shrikes are a common bird in this habitat during the spring and summer, scanning the ground below them for food. Woodlark can often be found here too, they are best looked for along the sides of tracks as they search for insects in the short vegetation.

The black, white and red plumage of the Woodchat Shrike makes this a very noticeable bird.

A wide range of raptors can be found hunting in this habitat, everything from huge Black Vultures through to the smaller Common Kestrel can be seen. Booted Eagles are common during spring and summer, ambushing the smaller birds with sudden stoops and dashes. Many areas of Cistus scrub have areas of bare ground within them and these provide sheltered basking spots for reptiles such as snakes. As a result it is a common sight to see the large Short-toed Eagle hovering over this habitat as it hunts these reptiles.

This habitat is a key component in the ongoing conservation efforts to save the Iberian Lynx, an animal that has the unenviable title of the most threatened cat in the world. Large amounts of money have been spent on restoring this habitat as well as on a captive breeding program. Progress has been slow, but, in the summer of 2014, captive bred Lynx were released into the wild in the region. It is hoped that these will boost the very small relict population leading to the reestablishment of the Lynx in the area.

> **BIRDING TIP!**
> Many Cistus dominated areas have stock grazing in them in low numbers. With the stock comes watering holes in the form of ponds dug into the ground. On hot days these are great places to watch for birds, especially seed eaters that need to drink regularly. They can be great places to see birds such as the Rock Sparrow which otherwise can be difficult to locate.

Red Deer and Wild Boar can also be found in this habitat, often lying up in the shady scrub on hot days. The Egyptian Mongoose, a species that was introduced to Spain by the Moors, can often be found during the daytime as it hunts through the undergrowth. Their presence is often given away by the alarm calls of small birds and by birds such as Azure-winged Magpies diving down at the scrub below them.

Cistus Scrub can be found throughout much of Extremadura; even small pockets on the edges of towns and villages are worth exploring. Monfragüe National Park has large areas of recently restored Cistus scrub and the Tajo International Natural Park also has very large areas of this excellent habitat. The area around Albuquerque in Badajoz province is also home to large expanses as is the Sierra de San Pedro to the north of the town.

Wetlands

Although not renowned for its wetlands, Extremadura is home to some extensive artificially created sites. Although created for purposes other than wildlife they have developed into real birding hotspots. One of the most extensive reed bed systems to be found in the region is found at Arrocampo, a shallow reservoir built to provide water for the nuclear power station at Almaraz in Cáceres province.

Arrocampo is home to a breeding colony of Black-crowned Night Herons.

Because the water level at Arrocampo has to be kept constant, it has allowed the reed beds to develop extensively and the site has now been giving the status of an Ornithological Park, complete with hides and an information centre in the village of Saucedilla (see Birding Areas section for more details).

A whole host of wetland species can be found here, with the stars perhaps being Purple Heron, Purple Swamphen and Little Bittern, all three of which are easy to see. Smaller birds are also an attraction with species such as Penduline Tit, Bearded Reedling, Savi's Warbler and even Moustached Warbler being found.

The Purple Swamphen often skulks in the reeds making an array of loud calls, but with a bit of patience, you should be rewarded with fine views.

The area is also attractive to raptors, with vultures regularly in the air as well as eagles and, in the spring and summer, dozens of Black Kite. The area is also home to a few pairs of Black-winged Kite. The star raptor here though is the Marsh Harrier, with large numbers breeding.

The other main wetland areas worth visiting are the large, artificially irrigated, rice growing areas. Although other sites exist, perhaps the most extensive and accessible area is around Madrigalejo and Vegas Altas on the Badajoz/Cáceres province border. In the winter the area is full of Common Crane providing a real birding spectacle, Greylag Geese also winter here in vast numbers as do numerous other wetland species. The winter is also a good time to look for Black-winged Kites that form small dormitories here and can be easy to see at this time of year.

Large flocks of small birds can be found, including the exotic Red Avadavat and Common Waxbill that have become naturalised and established themselves in large numbers. Spanish Sparrows abound, their noisy, tightly packed flocks being a real feature of the area.

Large flocks of Spanish Sparrow can be found in the rice growing areas.

These areas are good for wintering Marsh harrier with a winter roost recently reported near the village of Vegas Altas that consisted of over 500 birds. The winter also brings Merlin to the areas and they are often seen dashing at high speed, hunting the many small birds to be found. Other raptors are frequent too, with vultures drifting over on a regular basis. The rice growing areas can also attract rare visitors; recent ones include Pallid Harrier and Red-knobbed Coot.

At all the wetland sites invertebrates are common; the dragonflies are particularly well represented as are butterflies. Mammals too can be seen, with the Otter perhaps being the star, often showing itself in the daylight. They are particularly fond of the American Crayfish which can be found in abundance in the irrigation channels, look for otter spraints, full of their shells, strategically placed as adverts to other Otters.

> **BIRDING TIP!**
> Although found in other areas in Extremadura, the Black-winged Kite can be found all year round at Arrocampo and especially in the winter at the rice fields near Vegas Altas. Many people head for home as the light begins to fade, but this is the best time to see these small raptors. In the heat of the summer this is when they hunt and, in the winter, when they can form small groups – often on telegraph wires – prior to roosting. Staying out that bit longer can be rewarding.

Reservoirs

There are two types of reservoir found in Extremadura; shallow smaller ones, that provide water for towns and villages and huge ones created for Hydroelectric schemes.

Smaller, shallow town and village reservoirs, such as this one at Membrio, can hold good species.

Of the two, it is the smaller ones that can hold the most species. Not all are suitable, but the ones which have areas of scrub (often around the dam end) and areas of bare mud around the edges, can hold everything from warblers to waders. These sites are often very accessible with perimeter tracks allowing residents to have their evening walk around them. This can lead to disturbance, but it can also allow you great access to the site.

The dam end of the reservoir usually has an abundance of lush scrub growing around or below it. This can be a real magnet for species such as the Cetti's Warbler and the Nightingale, as well as numerous other small birds including Melodious Warbler. If the area is big enough, it can even support Golden Orioles. The cool shade that these areas provide can often be full of birds in the heat of the summer.

The 'cola' (meaning 'tail') end of the reservoir where the water enters, can often be the zone where most bare mud is exposed. This should be checked for waders, with different species being present at different times of year. One that is present all year around is the graceful and elegant Black-winged Stilt, probably the star bird of the small town or village reservoir.

The incredibly long legged Black-winged Stilt, this one with three chicks, is a common town reservoir bird.

These reservoirs can also be good for passage species moving through, with Avocet and other waders sometimes appearing for just a day or two before moving on. Other passage species stop for several weeks and of these, the Osprey is perhaps the main attraction. Many of these reservoirs are stocked with fish for local fisherman and these provide an irresistible stock of easy food for these large raptors.

Dragonflies are often very common, as are butterflies and numerous different types of beetle; these sites can keep an amateur entomologist busy for days!

The beautiful Red Veined Dragonfly can often be found alongside the shallower reservoirs.

The many hydroelectric dams and their reservoirs, created along the main river systems of the Tajo and Guadiana rivers, resemble elongated lakes. They are huge, the Tajo International, for example, is the second largest reservoir in Europe at over 90kms long. At first look, these reservoirs can look good for all sorts of water birds, but unfortunately they are often not. They are very deep and steep sided and, because the water levels fluctuate massively throughout the year, they have very little or no marginal vegetation.

Despite this though they are worth a look, especially where low islands are formed. These islands can provide breeding sites for birds such as the Collared Pratincole and Gull-billed Tern in the spring and summer, whilst in the winter they hold vast roosts of wintering Lesser Black-backed and Black Headed Gulls. Post breeding flocks of duck will also accumulate on these reservoirs whilst they moult their flight feathers.

The huge dams themselves often have incredibly large colonies of Crag and House Martins breeding on them and in winter have been known to play host to the occasional wintering Wallcreeper.

The vast amount of water is, of course, attractive to thirsty mammals, on hot days it is not infrequent to see Red Deer and even the normally nocturnal Wild Boar, drinking at their edges. Otters can also be seen frequently.

The smaller town/village reservoirs can of course be found across the region. Not all are suitable, but those that are can produce good close views of many species as they are often more used to human presence.

> **BIRDING TIP!**
> At weekends and fiestas the small reservoirs located close to towns and villages can be extremely busy with walkers and fisherman. The disturbance they cause can be tremendous so it is best to visit these sites during the working week when they are likely to be empty of people and hopefully full of birds.

The two main rivers that flow through Extremadura, the Tajo in Cáceres province and the Guadiana in Badajoz province, are the location for most of the large reservoirs (or embalses in Spanish). The Embalse de Valdecañas, on the Tajo can hold breeding colonies of both the Gull-billed Tern and Collared Pratincole. The Embalses de Orellana and La Serena in Badajoz province also hold large colonies of Gull-billed Tern and a colony of the Little Tern which is a rare breeder in Extremadura.

A Little Tern hovering over a reservoir as it hunts for fish.

Other large reservoirs in the region worth checking out include the Embalse de Alange and the newly established Embalse de Alcollarin, both in Badajoz province and the Embalse de Portaje in Cáceres province.

River Valleys

Steep sided river valleys, like the Rio Salor close to Membrio, offer great birding opportunities.

The smaller rivers that feed the two main rivers of the region are great locations for bird watching. They are often in steep sided valleys that provide great habitat for a number of species including Golden Eagle, Bonelli's Eagle, Eagle Owl, Black Stork, Rock Bunting, Blue Rock Thrush and Black Wheatear. Vultures will often be found making use of the up currents of air that the bare rocks and steep sides generate, sometimes getting very close to you as they do so.

The Golden Eagle is an iconic bird and one that often breeds in this habitat, spending time in the river valleys will help you connect with this large raptor. The subspecies here is slightly smaller and darker than the northern European race but otherwise is exactly the same in appearance and habits. They can often be seen aggressively driving off Griffon Vultures near their nesting areas, especially at the beginning of the year.

The Egyptian Vulture is a spring and summer visitor to the region, although a few do now over winter as well. It can be found breeding in some valleys and is often seen frequenting others, its distinctive silhouette making it stand out from the other raptors even at a distance.

The Egyptian Vulture has a wedge shaped tail that appears almost translucent against the sky.

The rivers are also home to Kingfishers and are often frequented by sandpipers, both Green and Common, as well as Little Ringed Plovers at varying times of year. The steep rocky slopes normally have Rock Bunting on, as well as Blue Rock Thrush and Black Wheatear. The latter have declined in recent years, but are still present in many of the steep sided river valleys, they can be shy but are always active, and, if present, should be easy to detect.

In the spring, following high water levels in the winter, many flowers appear alongside the river including the beautiful endemic irises of the region.

The month of September is a month when there are a lot of small birds present in the valleys; most of these birds are stopping off for a few weeks as they head south for the winter. Pied Flycatchers in particular, can be extremely common at this time, but you can also find other species such as Ring Ouzel, which only stop for a day or two.

In the scrubbier areas warblers abound, with Dartford Warbler and Sardinian Warbler that are present all year, being joined by birds such as Subalpine Warbler in the spring and summer. This scrub can also be a good place to see the Spanish race of Long-tailed Tit.

Otters are often present and can often be seen in the day if the area is quiet. The valleys are also often frequented by Red Deer as well. As the light goes at the end of the day it can also be possible to see Beech Marten and Polecat surreptitiously making their way down to the water for a drink before prowling the valley sides for prey.

Iberian Terrapins and their close relative the European Pond Terrapin can be frequently found basking on rocks at the side of the river. Both species are wary and will drop off in to the water when disturbed. The Iberian Terrapin is associated more with running water than the European, however it can be difficult to tell the apart, especially when they are often muddy!

European Pond Terrapins basking on a rock in a river.

The Viperine snake is another reptile that is often found by, and in, rivers. It is closely related to the Grass Snake and although it resembles a viper in colouration, hence the common English name, it is not venomous. If you look down at a river and see a snake swimming across it, it is highly likely that it is a Viperine. The bigger adults can often be seen basking at the bottom in shallow water where they are still able to absorb the sun's rays, out of reach of most predators.

There are numerous river valleys that offer excellent wildlife watching opportunities. The Rio Salor west of Cáceres, the Rio Almonte from east of Trujillo to the south of Monroy and the Rio Magasca and Rio Tamuja between Trujillo and Cáceres are all good examples of steep sided river valleys in Cáceres province.

BIRDING TIP!
The road bridges that cross rivers in Extremadura are often home to large breeding colonies of Hirundines. The largest colony in the region has to be the House Martin colony on the bridge across the Rio Tajo in Monfragüe National Park. Also nesting on this bridge, and on many others, are Alpine Swift giving you a good chance to get close views of these large Swifts. Everything from Spanish Sparrow to Common Kestrel will breed on these man made structures so be sure to check them out.

Birding Areas to Explore

The Extremadura region is rich in habitat and birds, but like anywhere else in Europe it is constantly changing. New roads are built, trees are planted, trees are felled, disturbance levels change, crops change and livestock use change. All of this can have detrimental and beneficial effects on wildlife. Therefore, this isn't a traditional site guide telling you to stop at exact points, as these only reflect a moment in time that can be very different from the moment that you visit it. Instead, this section highlights areas for you to explore, the sort of landscape you will find and the target birds that you can see in these areas.

The target birds are listed in taxonomic order, those that have a (W) after their name are primarily wintering species and those with (S) are spring and summer visitors – see the monthly birding section for details on arrival and departure dates. Please note though that some summering species, such as Egyptian Vulture, are beginning to over winter in low numbers so there is still a possibility of seeing them in the winter. The birds listed as target species are the pick of the area's avifauna and are likely to be found in the habitats that you will encounter there. Many species, from the Azure-winged Magpie to the Griffon Vulture, are found throughout most of the region and are therefore not listed as target species for particular areas.

The maps relate to the excellent Michelin 576 map that covers Extremadura. It is strongly recommended that you have a copy with you.

Birding Area 1: Arrocampo

A nuclear power station doesn't necessarily sound the most attractive of locations to go bird watching, but, because of the power station at Almaraz, the area surrounding it has developed into a fantastic birding site offering the visitor to Extremadura great opportunities to see birds that would otherwise be very hard to see in the region.

The shallow warm water is extensively colonised by well developed reed beds and this, in turn, has allowed a large avifauna to develop.

The area is very close to the A5 and EX A1 motorways and is therefore very easily accessed. It is perfectly situated for travellers that are coming from Madrid meaning that it can be comfortably visited as part of your journey to and from the airport.

The village of Saucedilla is the start point for this area, a small wooden information centre can be found on the southern edge of it and it is here that you need to go to collect the key for the hides that are dotted around the area. The site is very rich and you don't need to go to the hides to see many of the species present but, if you have time, the hides are well worth visiting.

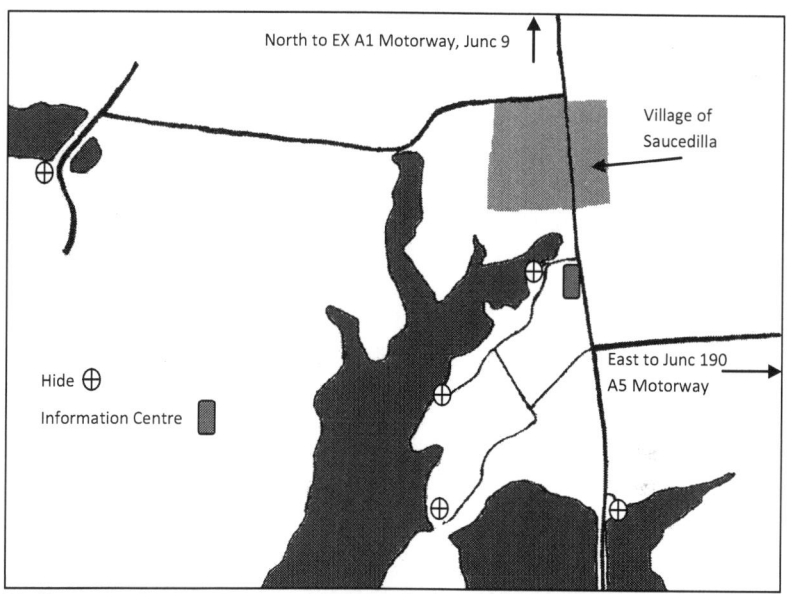

Birding Area 1 Map: Arrocampo – the dark grey areas depict the main areas of open water and reed beds

The area is very flat, lying between the towering Sierra de Gredos range to the north and the Villuercas range to the south. It is situated very close to the non accessible Eastern end of Monfragüe National Park and alongside a large area of dehesa called Campo Arañuelo. Much of the soil is very sandy, a wide variety of specialist plants can be found growing in the areas between the three hides that are situated between the reed beds and the information office.

The area is rich in bird life, the combination of open water, reed beds, nearby dehesa and the proximity of Monfragüe, make this an outstanding site for a days bird watching with a large variety of species possible. The main target species for this area are as follows, many more species, typical of Extremadura can also be seen here, with many raptor species frequently seen overhead.

> **BIRDING TIP!**
> Collect a key for the hides early in the day as there are only a limited number available. They will also give you a map with the hides shown on them. Of the five hides, hides 1, 2 and 4 are the best, the other two are situated poorly and you do not need to be in them to experience the birds present at their sites.

Arrocampo Target Species:

Little Bittern; Bittern (W); Night Heron; Squacco Heron (S); Great Egret; Purple Heron (S); Black Shouldered Kite; Marsh Harrier; Lesser Kestrel (S); Purple Swamphen; Common Crane (W); Black-winged Stilt; Gull-billed Tern (S); Whiskered Tern (S); Great Spotted Cuckoo (S); Sand Martin (S); Bluethroat (W); Moustached Warbler; Cetti's Warbler; Savi's Warbler (S); Great Reed Warbler (S); Bearded Tit; Penduline Tit; Tree Sparrow.

Birding Area 2: Taláván, Monroy and Santa Marta de Magasca

This area contains steppe, dehesa, Cistus scrub, small and large reservoirs and steep sided river valleys. With this collection of good habitat come a very good collection of bird species. It is particularly good for the steppe species such as Great and Little Bustard and both Sandgrouse.

It is easily accessed from either the A66 motorway or the A58 motorway that runs from Cáceres to Trujillo. There are a number of minor roads running through the area and all of these should be explored to maximise your chances of seeing the main target species.

The most productive and accessible areas of steppe lie around the small village of Santa Marta de Magasca and on the road that runs from the EX208 just to the north of Trujillo that heads for Monroy. The best areas of dehesa lie to the north of the EX390 particularly from the north of Monroy to the village of Torrejon el Rubio. There are lots of areas of Cistus scrub and these should be explored as and when you come across them. The small reservoir south of Taláván on the CC41 has two hides at either end of it and these are well worth a visit, whilst the large Embalse de Guadiloba reservoir to the east of Cáceres is a must visit site giving opportunities for water birds as well as access to more steppe. The steep sided valleys of the Rio Almonte, Rio Tamuja and Rio Magasca provide excellent examples of this type of habitat, all three of which can be accessed from the minor roads running through the area.

The area is very close to the accessible part of Monfragüe and many people only spend a cursory visit here on their way to and from the National Park. But this is an area that should be explored thoroughly though and at least a day is needed. Along with the target species you will see many more species typical of Extremadura.

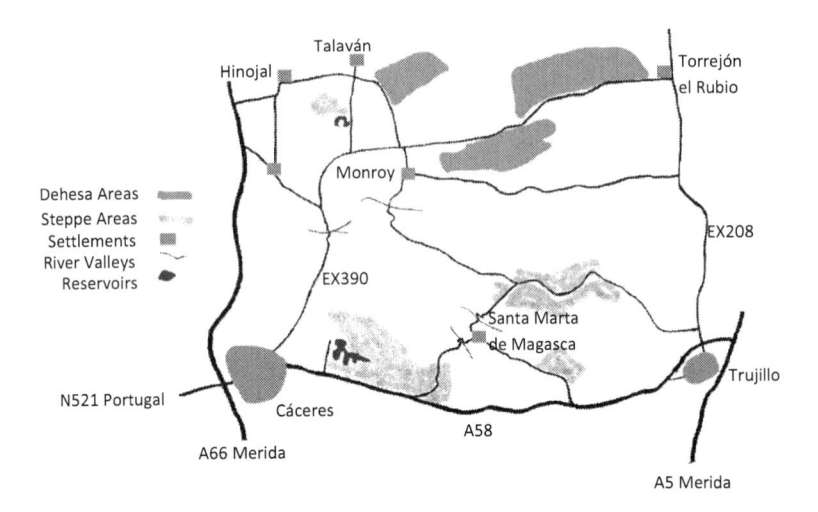

Birding Area 2 Map: The A58 motorway that runs between Cáceres and Trujillo runs parallel and entwined with the old road. The old road is now virtually traffic free and provides access to several tracks that lead north into the steppe between Cáceres and the turn off for Santa Marta de Magasca.

Talavan, Monroy and Santa Marta de Magasca Target Species:

Egyptian Vulture (S); Black Vulture; Black Shouldered Kite; Hen Harrier (W); Montagu's Harrier (S); Golden Eagle; Short-toed Eagle (S); Bonelli's Eagle; Lesser Kestrel (S); Merlin (W); Common Crane (W); Little Bustard; Great Bustard; Stone Curlew; Collared Pratincole (S); Golden Plover (W); Black-bellied Sandgrouse; Pin-tailed Sandgrouse; Great Spotted Cuckoo (S); Eagle Owl; Little Owl; Red-necked Nightjar (S); Alpine Swift (S); Bee-eater (S);

Roller (S); Hoopoe; Calandra Lark; Short-toed Lark (S); Woodlark; Black Wheatear; Black-eared Wheatear (S); Western Orphean Warbler (S); Rock Sparrow; Hawfinch

> **BIRDING TIP!**
> Looking for Great Bustard from the roadside can be productive, but these are wary birds and will avoid areas that attract too many people. Track entrances that don't have shut gates across them can generally be accessed. Walking just 100m along one of these will give you views of the steppe that you otherwise won't have and will maximise your chances of seeing these magnificent birds. Whenever you are leaving your vehicle though, ensure that it is not blocking anybody's access as no matter how remote the site seems it will be someone's way of getting to and from work or home.

Birding Area 3: Brozas, Alcántara and the Northern Sierra de San Pedro

The area contains steppe, dehesa, cistus scrub, small reservoirs, a large reservoir, a steep sided river valley and a range of low rocky hills. With this variety of habitat comes a good variety of bird life to be found. The Sierra de San Pedro has more breeding Spanish Imperial Eagles and Black Vultures than anywhere else in Extremadura.

The area is best accessed from the N521 Cáceres to Portugal road. Although the Sierra de San Pedro lies mainly on the south of this road only the area to the north of it is described. The southern part of the range is mainly covered by vast private estates which are closed to the public, although a number of roads cross this part of the range stopping opportunities are few and far between.

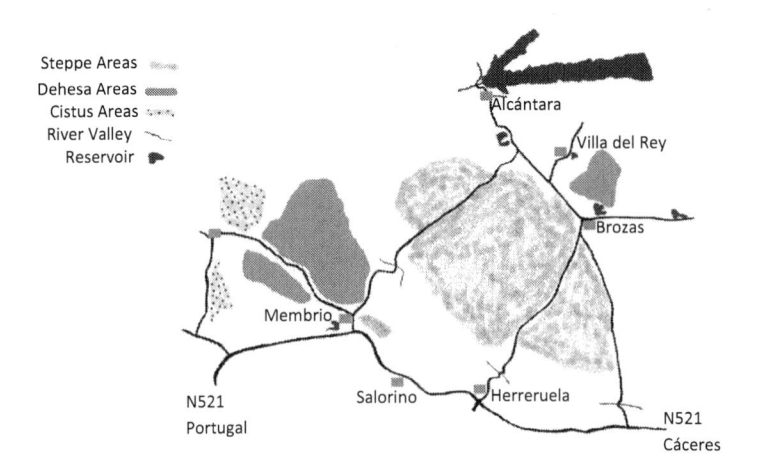

Birding Area 3 Map

The main part of Steppe lies between the town of Brozas and the village of Membrio with the EX117 and EX302 crossing the majority of it, there are several tracks running from these roads

> **BIRDING TIP!**
> Don't be afraid of exploring the urban environment as it can be home to some great species. Barn Owls are particularly common in the older towns and villages and Scops Owls regularly breed in the amenity trees that are planted there. In this area, both the towns of Brozas and Alcántara have large and nationally recognised breeding populations of Lesser Kestrel on their main churches – definitely worth a look!

deep into the habitat enabling you to get right to the heart of it. Large areas of dehesa can be found to the north of Brozas and to the north of Membrio, as with the steppe, there are a number of tracks that access this habitat and these should be explored. Cistus scrub can be found in many places with the best areas being found in the Sierra de San Pedro. There are a number of small reservoirs scattered across the zone but the most productive are the two situated close to Brozas. One of the largest reservoirs in Europe forms the northern boundary to this area; it can be best viewed from around the town of Alcántara. The Rio Salor is at its most productive in this area and is best viewed from just north of Membrio on the EX117 and just north of Herreruela on the EX302. The Sierra de San Pedro's low range of rocky hills can be best accessed from the roads that run between Membrio and Santiago de Alcantara.

Brozas, Alcántara and the Sierra de San Pedro Target Species:

Black Stork (S); Egyptian Vulture (S); Black Vulture; Hen Harrier (W); Montagu's Harrier (S); Spanish Imperial Eagle; Golden Eagle; Short-toed eagle (S); Bonelli's Eagle; Lesser Kestrel (S); Merlin (W); Common Crane (W); Little Bustard; Great Bustard; Stone Curlew; Golden Plover (W); Black-bellied Sandgrouse; Pin-tailed Sandgrouse; Great Spotted Cuckoo (S); Barn Owl; Eagle Owl; Little Owl; Scops Owl (S); Red-necked Nightjar (S); Alpine Swift (S); White-rumped Swift (S); Turtle Dove (S); Bee-eater (S); Roller (S); Hoopoe; Calandra Lark; Short-toed Lark (S); Woodlark; Tawny Pipit (S); Black Wheatear; Black-eared Wheatear (S); Western Orphean Warbler (S); Golden Oriole (S); Rock Sparrow; Hawfinch; Cirl Bunting

Birding Area 4: Monfragüe National Park

Monfragüe is a world famous birding destination and rightly so. It has a tremendous avifauna and although all of the species present can be seen in many other areas of Extremadura the sheer scale of the habitat and the landscape is one that just has to be experienced. The National Park was only designated such in 2007 but it had been protected to a lesser extent since 1979. The vast majority of the Park is closed to public access but the 20% of it that is accessible provides ample opportunities to see the species that are present.

The Park follows the Tajo Valley east to west as well as part of the Tietar Valley and it's confluence with the Tajo. A rocky low mountain range runs along the southern bank of the Tajo, where the river cuts through this ridge a large rocky cliff towers above the river. Called Peña Falcon this rock face is one of *the* birding sites in Europe; dominated by a huge breeding colony of Griffon Vultures (although a larger one exists in the non accessible part of the Park) the viewing areas on the opposite bank always have people in them training their scopes on the rock face.

The Park is accessed via the EX208 Trujillo to Plasencia road, spend a day or two exploring this road and the minor one that runs to the east about halfway through the Park. Stopping at the many parking areas and viewing spots along them will enable you to see and enjoy the fabulous wealth of wildlife present.

Other than the rocky ridge and two dammed rivers, the main habitat here is Cistus scrub, a recent large restoration project has successfully restored large areas of this habitat back to its

> **BIRDING TIP!**
> A small area of Pine forest can be found in the Park, the vast majority of visitors ignore this as they drive to the famous cliff sites to watch raptors, but this is a habitat worth investigating and a short stop here should reward you with Short-toed Treecreeper, Turtle Dove in the summer, the Spanish race of Long-tailed Tit and Crested Tit among many other species of small bird.

prime. A small settlement called Villarreal de San Carlos has numerous information outlets and displays as well as places to eat and some typical souvenir shops. The Park is very busy on Sundays and Holidays and parking at Peña Falcon at these times can be very difficult.

The rocky cliffs along the course of the two dammed rivers in the Park rightly attract the most attention from bird watchers. Alongside the numerous Griffon Vultures these cliff faces also have Egyptian Vulture, Black Stork, Eagle Owl, Peregrine Falcon, Raven, Blue Rock Thrush, Black Wheatear and Rock Bunting nesting on them. Crag Martins and Red-rumped Swallows also breed on these rocky faces and these are joined by Alpine Swift and White-rumped Swift. Peña Falcon is the main cliff site but there are several others worth checking including the La Tejadilla picnic site and the Portilla de Tietar both of which are on the Rio Tietar. The latter of these two offers the best chance of both Eagle Owl and Spanish Imperial Eagle. The Cistus scrub dominates throughout and there are a number of walking routes radiating out from Villarreal de San Carlos that will take you through this habitat giving great chances of seeing many of the warbler species associated with it. Maps showing the main cliff sites and the walks are available from the information centre in Villarreal. The two dammed rivers don't hold a lot of life, they are very deep and the levels change daily so there is no marginal vegetation, however Otters can be seen and in hot weather other mammals such as Wild Boar can be seen drinking from the edges.

A very large range of species can be seen and the area can also be good for passage birds at certain times of the year.

Monfragüe National Park Target Species:

Black Stork (S); Egyptian Vulture (S); Black Vulture; Spanish Imperial Eagle; Short-toed eagle (S); Bonelli's Eagle; Sparrowhawk; Peregrine Falcon; Eagle Owl; Little Owl; Scops Owl (S); Red-necked Nightjar (S); Alpine Swift (S); White-rumped Swift (S); Turtle Dove (S); Bee-eater (S); Hoopoe; Black Wheatear; Subalpine Warbler (S); Western Orphean Warbler (S); Crested Tit; Short-toed Treecreeper; Hawfinch

Birding Area 5: Vegas Altas and La Serena

The two very different birding sites of the Vegas Altas rice fields and the La Serena steppe are very close to one another allowing them to be both explored in the one visit. In addition to these two habitats, the area also has two very large reservoirs, the Embalse de Orellana and the Embalse de la Serena.

Although slightly removed from many of the main bird watching spots in the region it is easily accessed via the EX335 and the N430. La Serena is accessed via a number of smaller roads with the principle road being the BA35 which runs right through the middle of this steppe area.

From north of the town of Madrigalejo a massive area of artificially irrigated rice fields begins. It is a vast complex with many tracks crossing it, all of which can give you access to potential sites. Perhaps the most compact and easily navigated area is south of the small town of Vegas Altas. Different times of the year, different stages of crop growth and different water levels can all affect where it is best to look. Avoid areas where obvious work is taking place as this causes disturbance, but with it being such a large area you are bound to find good sites.

South of this area lie the two large reservoirs, both have areas below the dams that are accessible by car and both have very well developed scrub communities making them valuable wildlife habitat in their own right. South of these reservoirs lies the open steppe that is called La Serena, the BA35 runs across the middle of this area and provides several stopping points as well as access to a number of tracks that should be explored. This is a large expanse of steppe and can seem empty at times but it holds large numbers of both Bustards and both Sandgrouse making it a must visit destination for the birder.

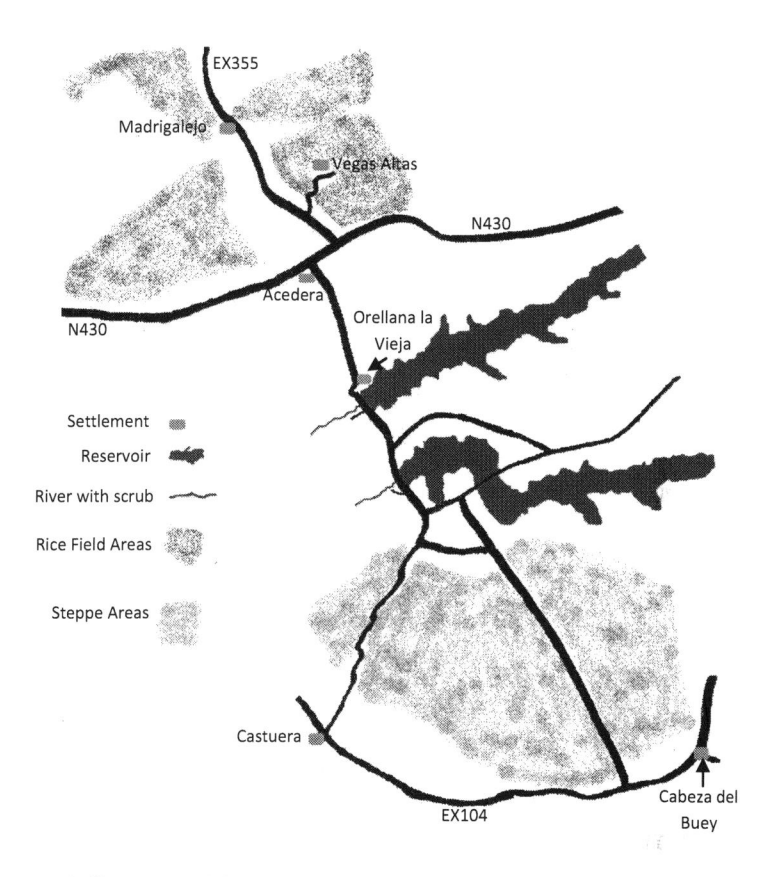

Birding Area 5 Map

> **BIRDING TIP!**
> After breeding, duck species moult their flight feathers rendering them unable to fly. The large Embalse de Orellana plays host to a large gathering of Red-crested Pochard that shelter there during the moult in June and July. Numbers can reach 1500, so if you are in the region in early summer, this is a site to visit.

Vegas Altas and La Serena Target Species:

Red-crested Pochard; Black-shouldered Kite; Marsh Harrier; Hen Harrier (W); Montagu's Harrier (S); Water Rail; Common Crane (W); Little Bustard; Great Bustard; Avocet (W); Stone Curlew; Collared Pratincole(S); Kentish Plover; Little Stint (W); Ruff; Black-tailed Godwit (W); Gull-billed Tern (S); Little Tern (S); Whiskered Tern (S); Pin-tailed Sandgrouse; Black-bellied Sandgrouse; Bee-eater (S); Roller (S); Calandra Lark; Short-toed Lark (S)Tawny Pipit (S); Black-eared Wheatear (S); Red Avadavat; Common Waxbill

The Magnificent Seven

With such a fantastic avifauna, selecting just a few of the birds that can be seen in Extremadura is difficult. However, the birds that follow are truly iconic species of the region and are must see species for any birder that is visiting it. They are Extremadura's Magnificent Seven.

Black Stork

This slightly smaller relation of the much commoner White Stork is primarily a spring and summer species. That said, a handful of birds will over winter in the region, but it is not known whether these are birds that have bred elsewhere in Europe and have migrated to the region for the winter or are birds that bred in Extremadura.

The Black Stork is easily recognised with its black neck and head instantly telling it apart from the White Stork. The adults have a red bill and red legs but the juveniles have green bills and legs.

The breeding population in Extremadura is estimated to be about 200 pairs which is approximately 40% of the total Iberian population. The majority of these breed in Cáceres province, particularly along the Tajo valley and its tributaries. The south west of Badajoz province also holds a strong breeding nucleus. Just over half of these pairs breed on rocky cliff faces with steep sided river valleys being the favourite locations. The rest of the birds breed in tree nests, with large Cork Oaks being the favoured species used.

The birds are generally shy, flying away from you if spotted feeding and are mainly seen soaring on air currents, especially in river valleys. Peña Falcon in Monfragüe National Park is by far the best place to see these birds breeding with several pairs nesting in full view of the viewing areas.

Birding Areas 3, 4 and 5 are good places to see Black Stork.

Griffon Vulture

Although not a rare species in Extremadura, this large resident raptor is definitely an iconic one. It is a rare event indeed to have a blue sky that doesn't have one of these large raptors drifting across it.

In flight, at a distance and against a bright sky, it can only really be confused with the Black Vulture, but Griffons fly with their wings in a shallow 'V' shape and the trailing edge of the wing is more bulging than that of the Black. Closer to, it is immediately recognisable with a buff brown back and off white ruff, neck and head.

The breeding population in Extremadura has increased significantly in recent years with an estimated 2,000 or so breeding pairs. Over 40% of these pairs are found on the nesting cliffs in Monfragüe National Park. Cáceres is undoubtedly the main province for these birds in terms of breeding colonies with other strongholds further west along the Tajo, in particular around the Alcántara area, the Sierra de Gata and the north of the Sierra de San Pedro. The main breeding colonies in Badajoz are around Puerto Peña and the reservoir Embalse de Cijara.

Griffon Vultures wander huge distances in their search for food, so, even well away from the steep cliffs they favour for nesting, you are likely to see these birds. On the ground they are wary, but in flight they seem to lose their shyness and can often fly very close to you as they follow the air currents to perfection. The various nesting cliffs of Monfragüe offer the best opportunities for close observation of these birds at their nesting sites.

Birding Areas 1, 2, 3, 4 and 5 are all good places to see Griffon Vulture.

Black Vulture

Although much rarer than the Griffon Vulture the Black is easy to see in Cáceres province where almost 40% of the birds entire Western Palearctic population can be found. It is a massive bird, bigger than the Griffon Vulture, with a wingspan not far off three metres in length.

In flight, it holds the wings flat with the trailing edge virtually parallel with the front edge, giving a rectangular shape to the bird's silhouette. When seen on the ground, either loafing in ones or twos or in amongst hordes of Griffon Vultures at a carcass, the large size is immediately obvious. Unlike Griffon Vulture, the Black Vulture prefers to nest in large trees, particularly those growing on steep slopes.

Within the region, the two main core areas for the bird are the Sierra de San Pedro (which overlaps from Cáceres into Badajoz province) which has 336 pairs and Monfragüe National Park that has 287 pairs. Unlike the Griffons they are happy to descend and feed on much smaller carcasses including animals as small as Rabbits. Whilst likely to be found drifting through the air in many parts of Cáceres province some of the best views of these huge birds can be had on the steppe areas between Membrio and Brozas. The birds will often sit out on the steppe looking like huge black rocks enabling you to get good views.

Birding Areas 2, 3 and 4 are good places to see Black Vulture.

Spanish Imperial Eagle

For many, this is the must see bird in Extremadura. It is endemic to the Iberian Peninsula and is, therefore, found nowhere else in the world. Although closely related to the Eastern Imperial Eagle the Spanish is a separate species with notable plumage differences, particularly in the juvenile stages.

In flight it appears very dark, especially when compared to the Golden Eagle, the only species that you are likely to confuse it with. The white markings on the front edge of the wings are easily visible in good light, but against a bright sky they can be surprisingly hard to distinguish. Unlike the Golden, the Spanish Imperial lacks the bulging trailing edge to the wings giving them a more rectangular shape.

In the early 1970s these raptors were reduced to a total global population of just 50 breeding pairs. Thankfully, due to extensive conservation efforts, the total population is estimated to be nearly 400 pairs, all but a handful of these breeding in Spain with the remainder in Portugal. Extremadura is home to 53 breeding pairs with the Sierra de San Pedro having the greatest density of breeding pairs in the region.

The area between Membrio and Santiago de Alcántara in the west of Cáceres province offers great chances of seeing this bird as does the Portilla de Tietar in Monfragüe National Park.

Birding Areas 3 and 4 are good places to see Spanish Imperial Eagle.

Common Crane

In the winter a large percentage of the European population of Crane heads to the Iberian Peninsula. From late October to the beginning of March these graceful birds can be seen and heard across the region.

Very distinctive in flight, with its neck and legs outstretched, the birds can often be seen flying in loose lines, known as ribbons, or in 'V' shaped formation. Their flight call is far carrying, it's evocative sound alerting you to their presence often long before they come in to view.

Around half of the wintering birds in Spain winter in Extremadura. The wintering population of these birds in the region fluctuates, but in recent winters it has peaked over 100,000 individuals with an incredible 128,850 birds being recorded in December 2013. The vast majority of these are found in the artificially irrigated rice fields along the Guadiana valley. Over the winter, and particularly in February, the birds feed voraciously on acorns to build up their reserves for the migration back to their breeding grounds. Areas of dehesa can hold large numbers of these feeding birds at this time.

Found throughout the region, they are not hard to locate in the winter. However, one of the most spectacular birding sights in

Europe can be had on the Cáceres/Badajoz boundary south of the town of Madrigalejo and around the town of Vegas Altas. Here, on the large expanses of rice fields, tens of thousands of Cranes can be seen all around you and in the air above you. The noise from their calls is deafening and the sheer number of birds is spellbinding – a definite must see for any birder.

Birding Areas 2, 3 and 5 are good places to see Common Crane.

Great Bustard

Like the Spanish Imperial Eagle, the Great Bustard is very high on the wish list of the birders that visit Extremadura. These large endangered birds are found on the many steppe areas of the region.

The Great Bustard is an unmistakeable bird, the males, which are much bigger than the females, stand at around one metre tall. Although capable of long sustained flight, the Great Bustard prefers to quietly walk away from sources of disturbance helping it to remain undetected. These are wary birds, but in the large open habitat of the Spanish steppe they can usually be found with a bit of effort.

Spain and Portugal are home to about 60% of the global population of this species, with the Spanish population numbering around 30,000 individuals. Extremadura is estimated to have a population of 6,500 birds.

The main areas to see these birds in Extremadura are the steppe habitats that can be found around Santa Marta de Magasca and Brozas in Cáceres province and the vast open land of La Serena and the Campiña Sur area in Badajoz province.

Birding Areas 2, 3 and 5 are good places to see Great Bustard.

Azure-winged Magpie

This beautiful corvid is a popular target species for many bird watchers. Highly gregarious, the noisy contact calls of this bird can be heard throughout many habitats. Although often thought to be introduced, recent fossil evidence has shown that this species of Magpie is in fact endemic to the Iberian Peninsula.

With its long tail and rounded wings the bird closely resembles the shape of the larger Common Magpie. The plumage, however, is completely different! With a combination of its black cap, pinkish brown back and blue wings and tail this is definitely an unmistakeable bird. Seen in good light it has to be one of Europe's prettiest birds.

The total world population of about a quarter of a million birds is found entirely in Spain and Portugal, with the core area of the bird's range being Cáceres province. It avoids open treeless landscapes such as steppe, but is likely to be found in almost any other habitat, especially favouring the dehesa habitat of Evergreen Oaks.

Although generally a wary bird, they have learnt that Humans can mean food, especially around picnic sites where they have been known to come in and perch on the table by you. Sites such as Monfragüe National Park in Cáceres province and Cornalvo Natural Park in Badajoz province are two such places where this can happen.

Birding Areas 2, 3 and 4 are good places to see Azure-winged Magpie.

The People and Life of Extremadura

Extremadura has about 1.1 million people living in it. This equates to 25 people per square kilometre which is very low when compared to the 407 people per square kilometre in England. Of those 1.1 million people, over one third of them live in 7 cities making the countryside even less populated. It is no coincidence that one of the least populated areas of Europe is also one of the best for bird watching.

Extremeños, as the people of Extremadura are known, can, at first glance, appear to be a taciturn bunch. They are, however, a friendly and highly gregarious people who like nothing better than socialising and discovering what it is that you are doing.

As you drive through a village or people drive past you, you will find that you are stared at intently. At first this can feel quite intimidating, indeed in Britain we would consider it rude, but in Extremadura it is perfectly normal. The culture in this wildlife paradise is very different to the culture of Britain.

Many of the people who live there don't know much about the rich wildlife they have, however, more and more people are showing interest and it is now not that unusual to find a Spanish birdwatcher, when a few years ago it was almost impossible. If you are out birding and have a telescope on something of interest and there are some Spaniards about, invite them to take a look at it, you will find them very appreciative of the opportunity.

Most villages will have a small general store and a chemist. These will open in the morning and close at 2pm before reopening around 5pm, often staying open to 8:30pm. On Saturdays most shops are only open until 2pm, on Sunday they are shut all day. All shops observe these type of hours other than the large supermarkets found in or near the larger population centres. These are open all day, but even they normally close earlier on a Saturday and they too are shut on a Sunday. These hours are typical for all types of businesses, including information offices and museums. One type of business that doesn't adhere to these hours are bars; they are open all day and long into the evening, including Sundays.

Most bars will serve you free tapas with your drink (although not with hot drinks normally), this can consist of anything from a few peanuts or olives through to Russian salad and cooked meat. In addition to this, most bars will do simple sandwiches known as Bocadillos and the larger ones will usually have a Raciones menu of simple bar food. It is normal not to pay for your drinks until you are about to leave, the bar staff will look at you oddly if you go to pay as they serve you!

Restaurants, especially in rural areas, don't open until 9pm – which is the time that most people eat their evening meal in the region. The menu del dia offers good value for money, usually consisting of a first and second course followed by a simple dessert and including bread and a drink.

There are numerous public holidays, and if these fall mid week they are normally linked to the weekend by dias de puente or bridging days. These are normally centred around religious festivals and happen throughout the year. The main religious festival is that of Easter or Semana Santa (Holy Week) as it is known in Spain. Easter is a very busy time in many rural villages and accommodation can be very difficult to find during it. Places like Monfragüe can also be extremely busy and noisy at this time too.

Driving in Extremadura and the Guardia Civil

Following a large investment of money spent on the road network in Extremadura during the late 1990s and early 2000s, many of the roads have been significantly improved. This means that the narrow, twisting, slow roads of old have mostly gone. It also means that the roads are now faster and that stopping on the side of them to watch birds is now a thing of the past. If the road you are driving on has a solid white line along it's edge, and most of the new roads do, you are not allowed to stop on them other than in an emergency. The rural police force, called the Guardia Civil, don't consider an unidentified bird as an emergency – more on them in a moment.

You are only allowed to stop on the side of the road where the line is dashed or non - existent. The new roads may have solid lines but they usually also have gateways and tracks joining them at regular intervals and, as long as you can get completely off the road, these can make great spots for a quick scan to see what is about.

The speed limit on open country roads will vary between either 90kmph (approx. 55mph) or 100kmph (approx. 60mph). If the road is particularly twisty, such as when dropping down into a river valley for example, then the limit may well be slower. A sign saying 30kmph (approx 20mph) means there is a hairpin coming up, so be warned!

Towns and villages have a 50kmph (approx. 30mph) limit and this is backed up in many cases with a traffic light system which detects (or perhaps decides!) that you are exceeding the speed limit and will turn the next set of lights to red. Virtually all villages with a main road going through them will have speed bumps, these can be particularly severe and definitely slow you down. Driving at night can be a good way of seeing mammals as well as picking up the occasional Eagle Owl sat on a roadside sign – I have seen several Eagle Owls like this. However, some of the mammals are big – Wild Boar and Red Deer for example – and are not necessarily used to traffic (the roads of Extremadura are pleasurably empty of traffic). It is therefore very important to keep your speed down and always be prepared for an animal to be on the road ahead of you – I have even had a herd of cows appear out of the darkness!

Drink driving is rightly frowned on and severely punished with a

> **BIRDING TIP!**
> When improving the road network, new bridges were built across the river valleys leaving the existing bridge redundant. Rather than these bridges being demolished they have been left and usually have access to them via a section of old road. These make great bird watching locations, they are off the road, have no traffic and enable you to spend as much time as you want watching the valley. In particular, these valleys are good for raptors and hirundines as well as for species such as Rock Bunting and Black Wheatear.

newly introduced **minimal** fine of €1,000 plus potential bans and jail sentences. Just don't do it.

The Guardia Civil are the police force that patrol rural Spain and you are bound to see them as you drive around Extremadura (they can often also be found in hotel bars in the morning enjoying a coffee!). They carry out random spot checks, usually basing themselves at junctions. These spot checks are frequent and for those not used to it can be intimidating. However, they are just doing their job and usually, once they know you are foreign, they will let you carry on after a minute or two. All the police in Spain carry guns and the Guardia Civil are no exception with pistols in holsters on their belts and sometimes bigger weapons in their hands. This is perfectly normal in Spain but obviously not in Britain and again can be intimidating for those not used to it. When driving in Spain you should always have your photo driving licence with you as they will ask to see it if you are stopped. Sometimes they will ask you a barrage of questions about where you are going and what you are doing etc. But just remember they are only doing their job.

They are sticklers for the rules of the road and can dish out on the spot fines for any offences that you may have been committing (not wearing a seatbelt for example). They certainly won't tolerate you stopped on the side of a solid white lined road watching birds and you can guarantee that they will turn up if you try!

About the Author

Ian Parsons worked for twenty years as a Ranger in Great Britain, working with some of Britain's rarest and most enigmatic species such as the Dormouse, European Nightjar and the Goshawk.

He now spends his time between his home county of Devon in the south west of England and his adopted home of Extremadura. A regular contributor to several magazines, including Bird Watching, Ian has also written other books including 'A Birding Miscellany' and a 'Journey Through a Birder's Thoughts' both of which are available on Amazon.

Ian and his wife Jo set up Griffon Holidays in 2012. Griffon Holidays organises and runs fantastic value for money bird tours to Extremadura, specialising in small groups of up to four people, ensuring that all participants on the tour get the very best experience of this wonderful region. Find out more at www.griffonholidays.com and follow Ian on twitter at @Birder_Griffon

Griffon Holidays

Printed in Great Britain
by Amazon